Coloring Books for Grown Ups

Creative Mandala Patterns for the Enthusiastic Artist

Ideal for Relaxation and Stress Relief

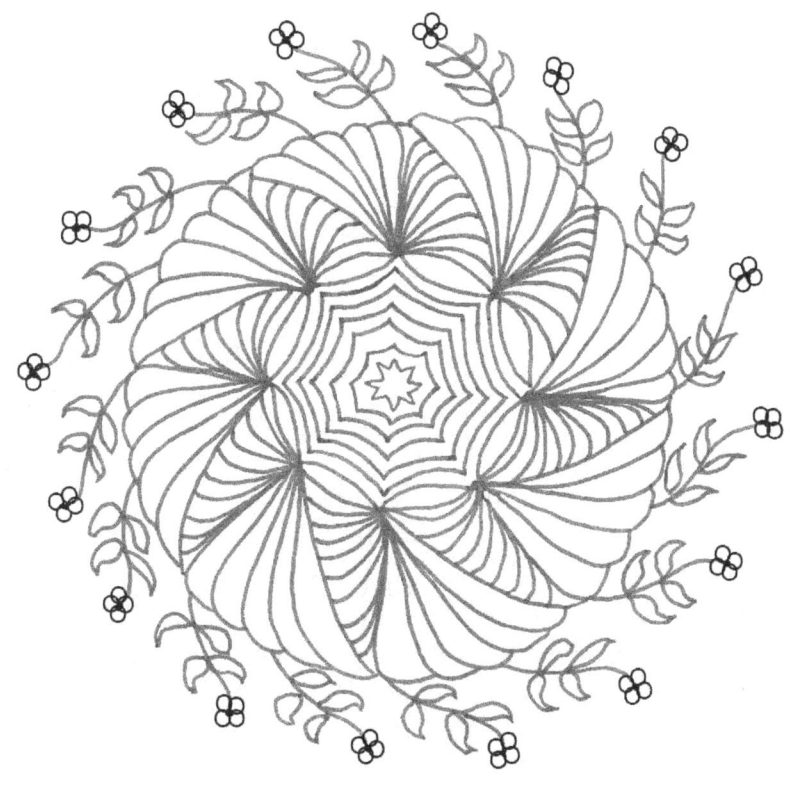

By: Kaye Dennan

KD Coloring Studio

ISNB: 978-1519733467

PUBLISHERS NOTES
Disclaimer

Paperback Edition

Manufactured in the United States of America

A note from the Illustrator

Creative Mandala Patterns for the Enthusiastic Artist

This book was developed especially for those who appreciate the shape, color and style of the various designs.

The wide range of images in this book will give you the chance to extend your capacity for working with color and shapes.

Discovering your inner artistic pleasure is one of life's happiest moments. It is a creative experience you can enjoy all on your own but one that you can share with others as well.

When you start coloring it is easy to color between the lines and find enjoyment just in the practice of adding color to paper.

As you continue in your discovery you will find that colors talk to each other, they mix and blend and create new emotions.

Colors speak to us too.

Become aware of the affect of colors on your emotions. Take the time to site and understand the change of emotions as you take in colors that you see. When outside look at different colors and recognize your emotion. Look at blocks of color and see if it makes any difference to the way you feel.

Most of us have favorite colors and they are favorites because we like how they make us feel when we see them or even wear them.

Some people even find that their observance of a color a person is wearing affects the way that they initially react to a person: positively, negatively or cautiously.

Basic relationships are listed below but the reality is that what might make one person feel cheerful can make another person feel irritated depending on the viewers' past experiences or cultural differences.

Warm Colors – Red, Orange, Yellow

Cool Colors – Green, Blue, Purple

Neutral Colors – Black, Gray, White, Tan, Brown

I encourage you to experiment with color and shapes and enjoy your coloring pass-time.

****

Every Second Page has been left blank so that you do not ruin one of your colored designs with color bleeding through the back.

If you are using pencils then I would suggest you slide a piece of thin cardboard or thick paper under the page you are color just to prevent any pressure marks on the following page.

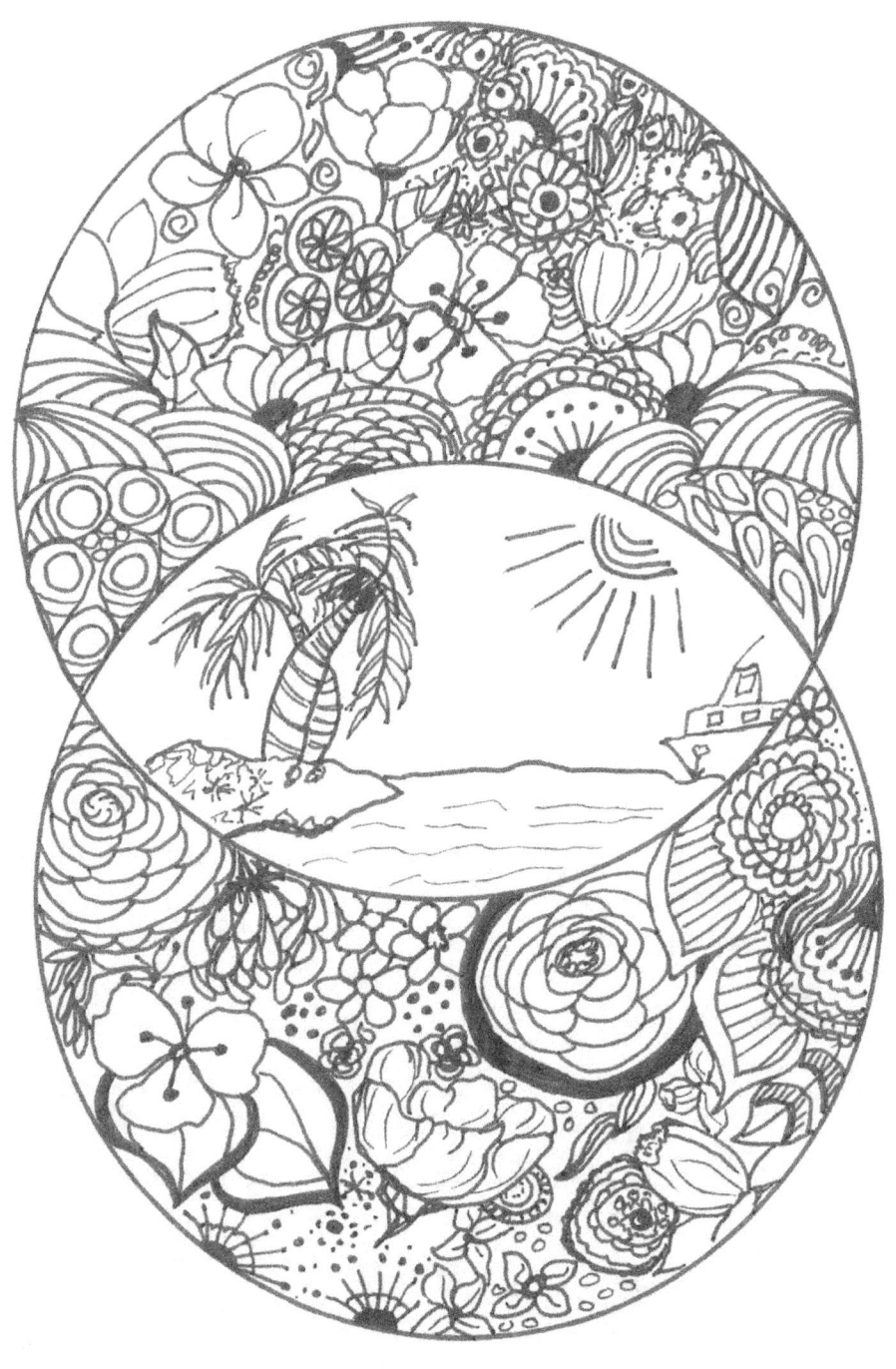

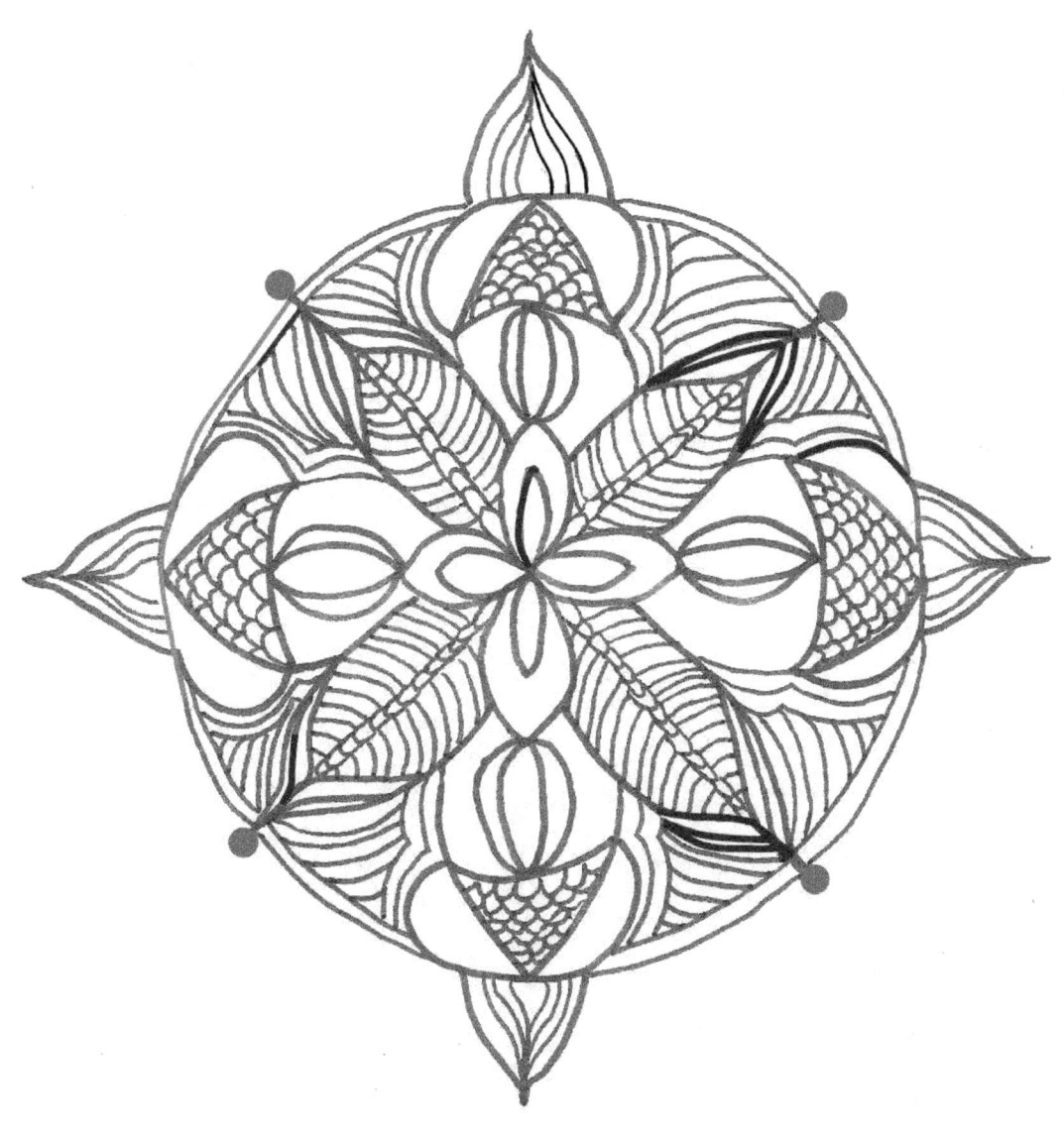

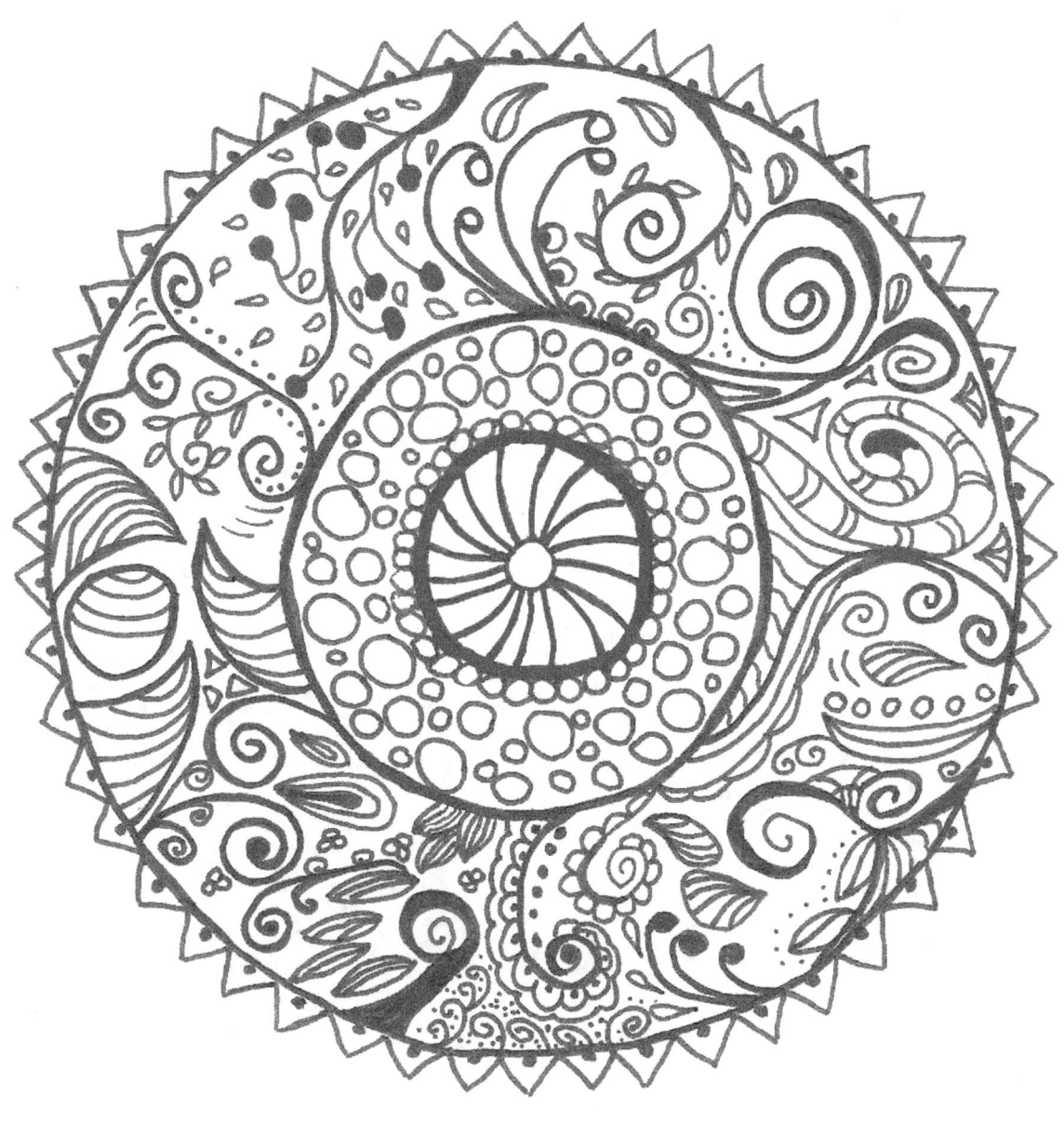

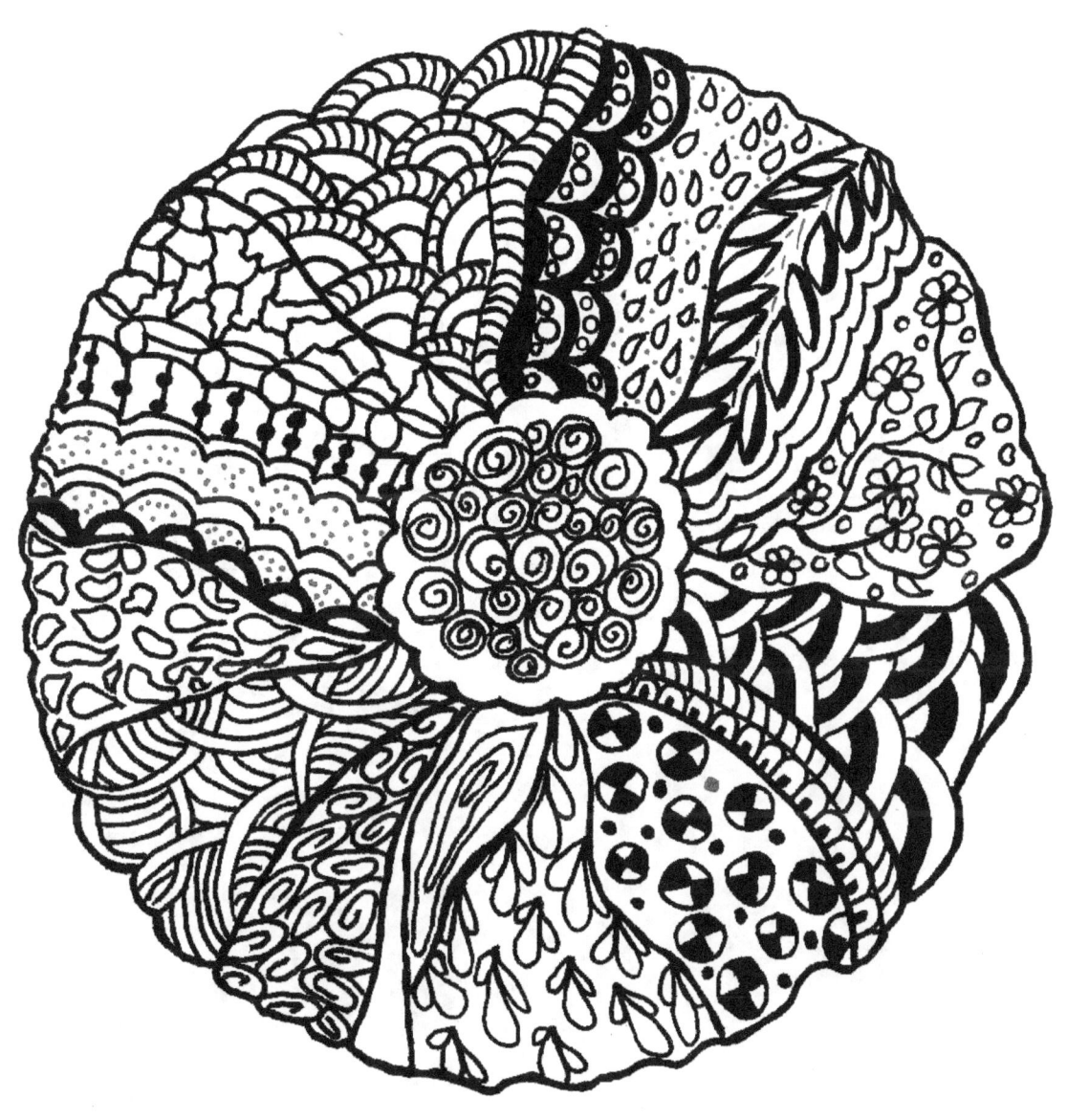

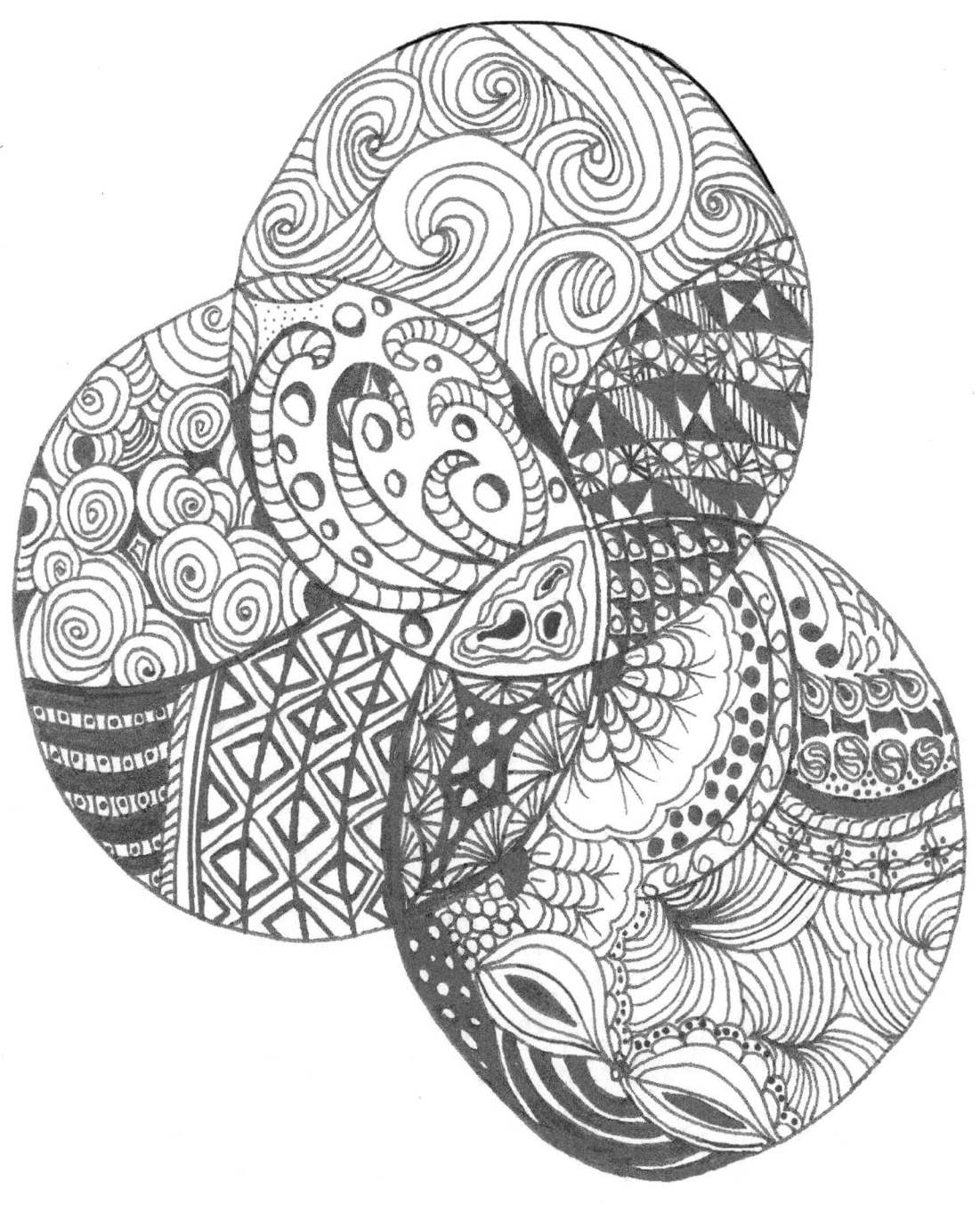

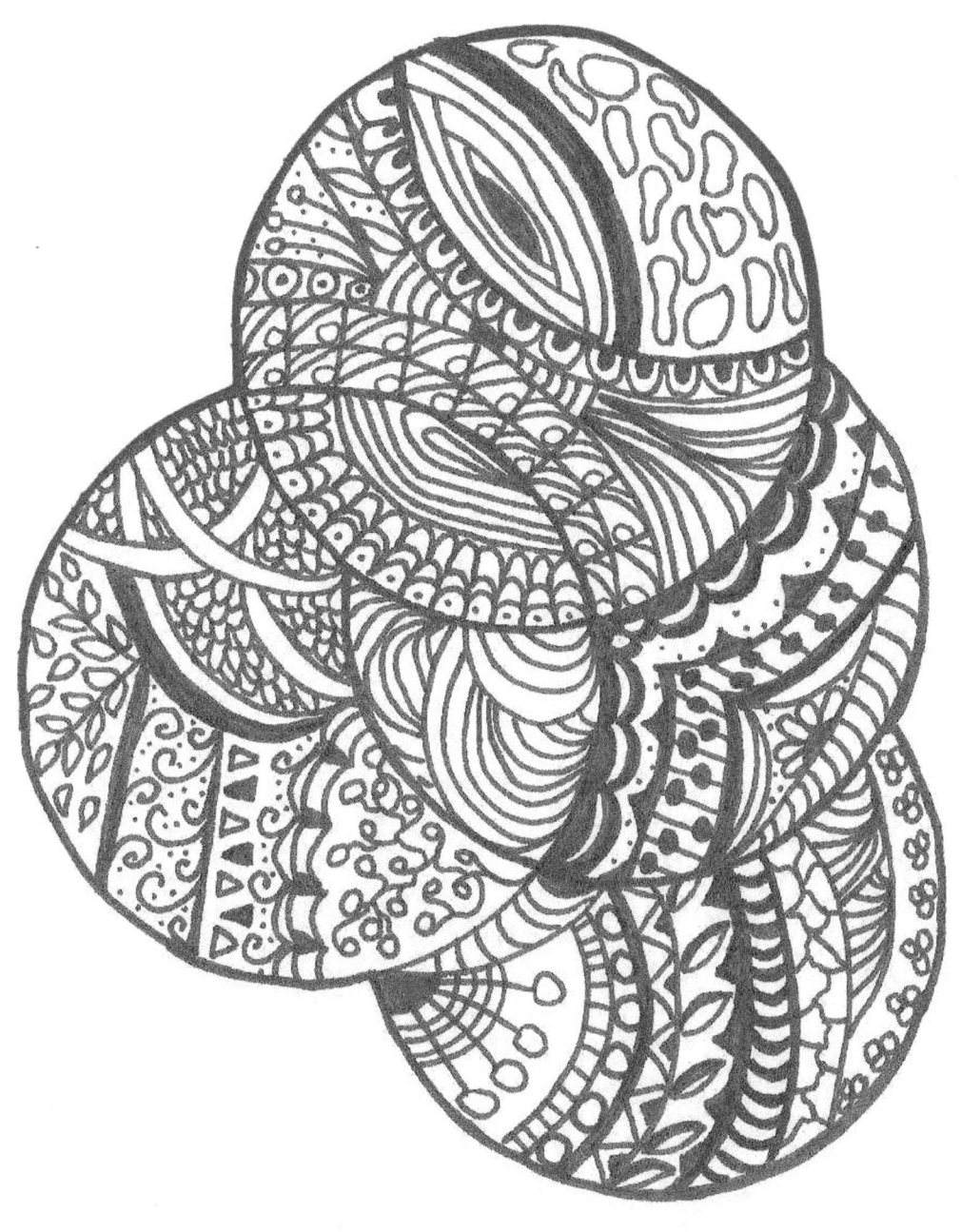

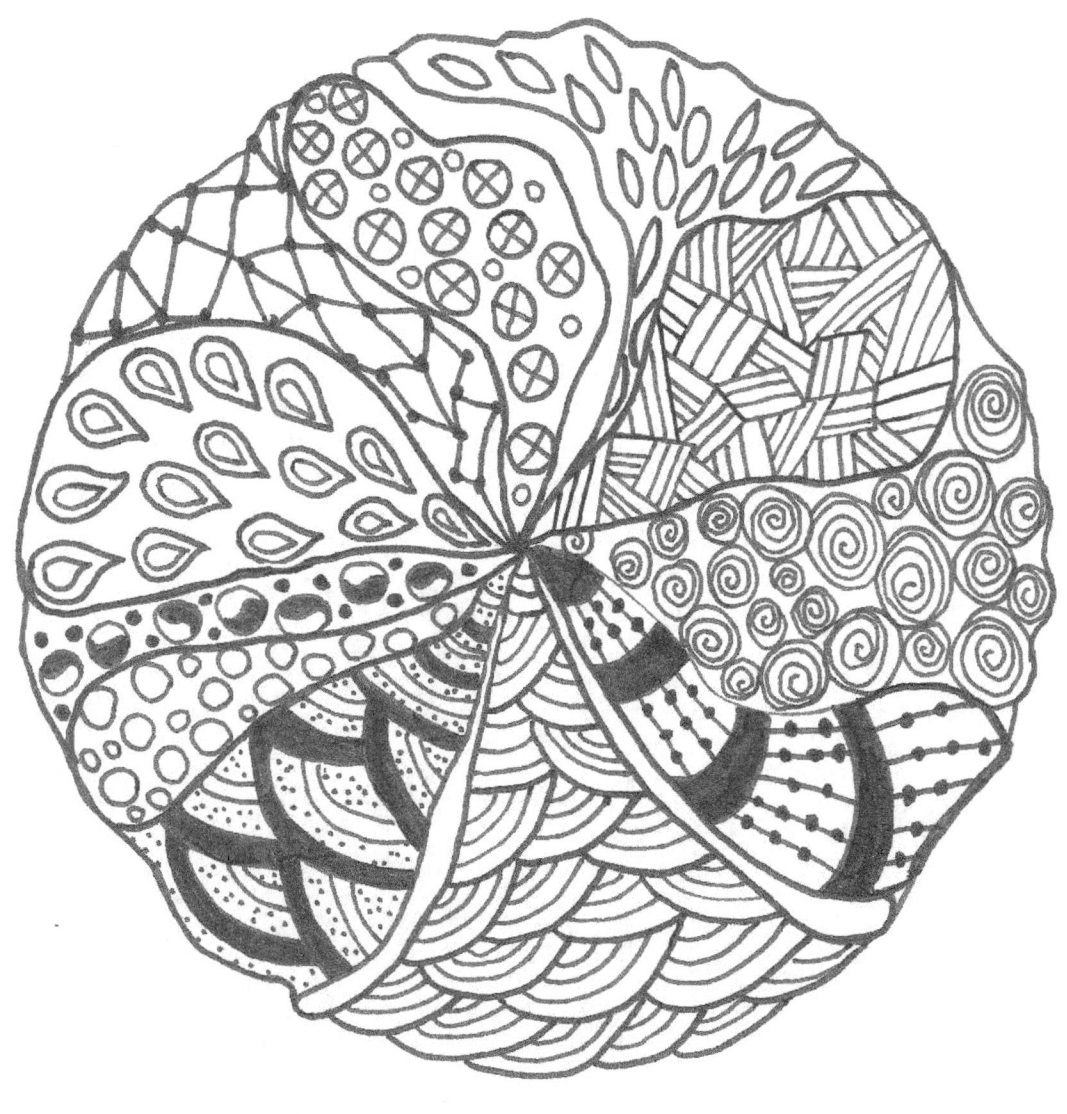

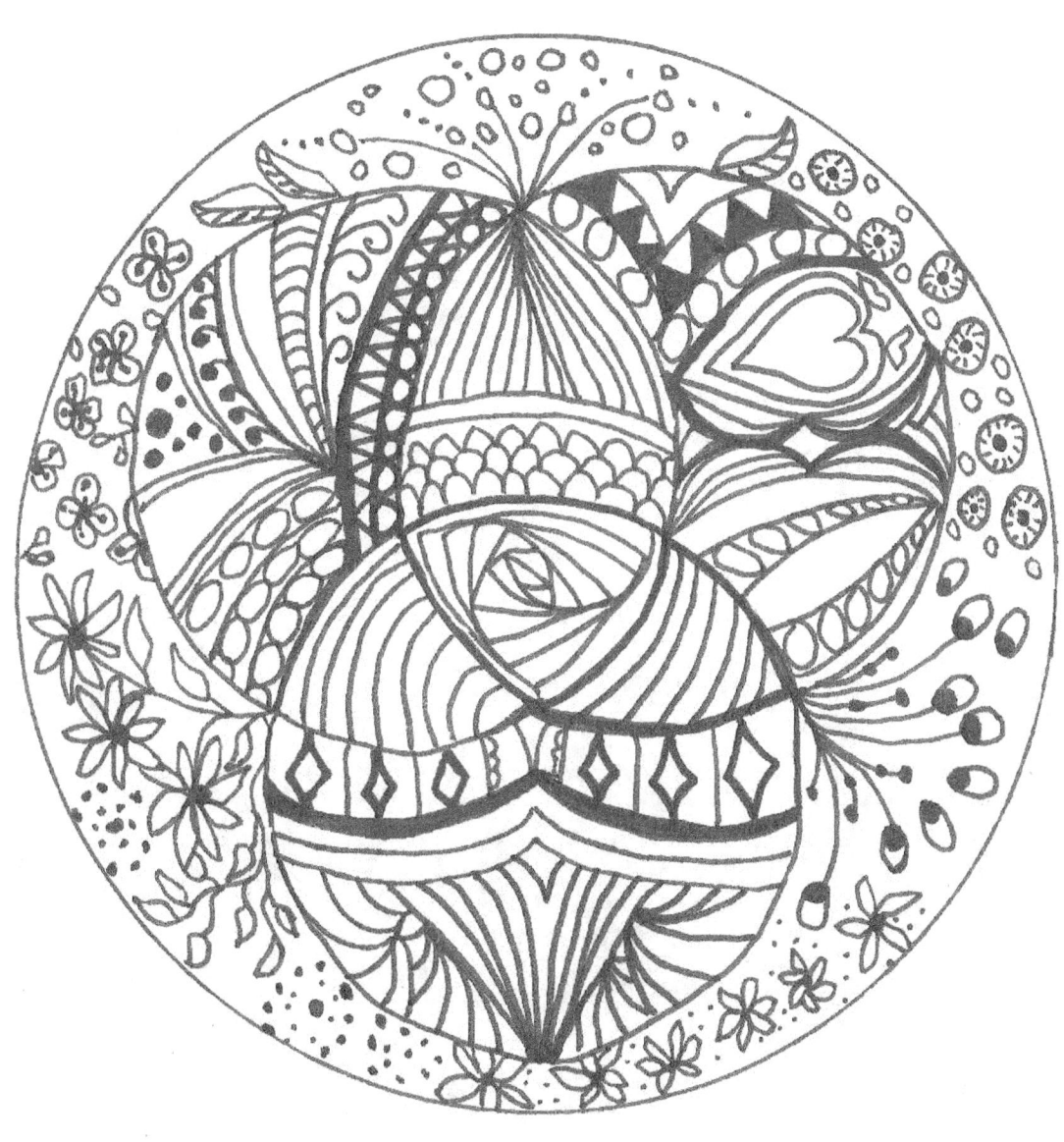

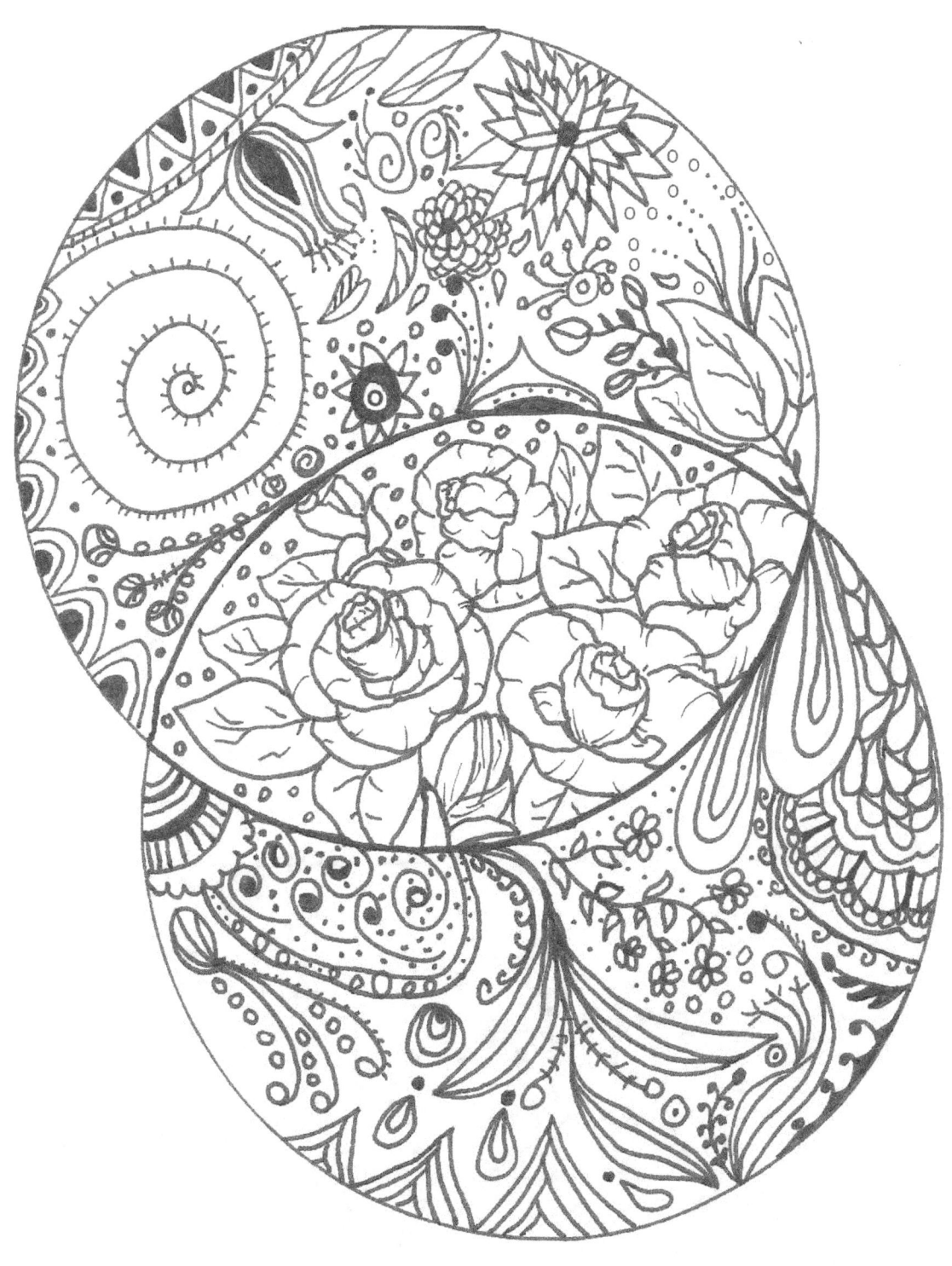

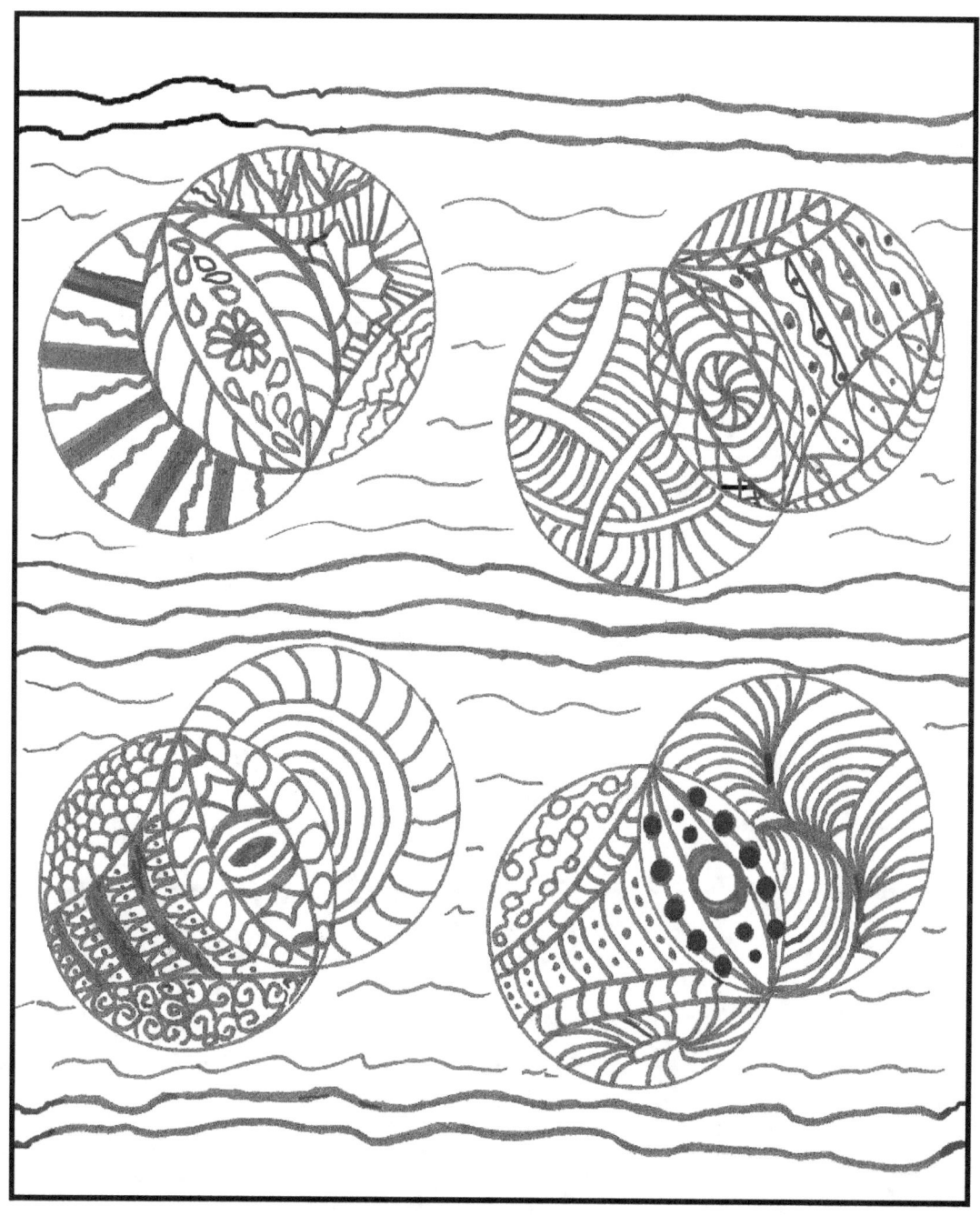

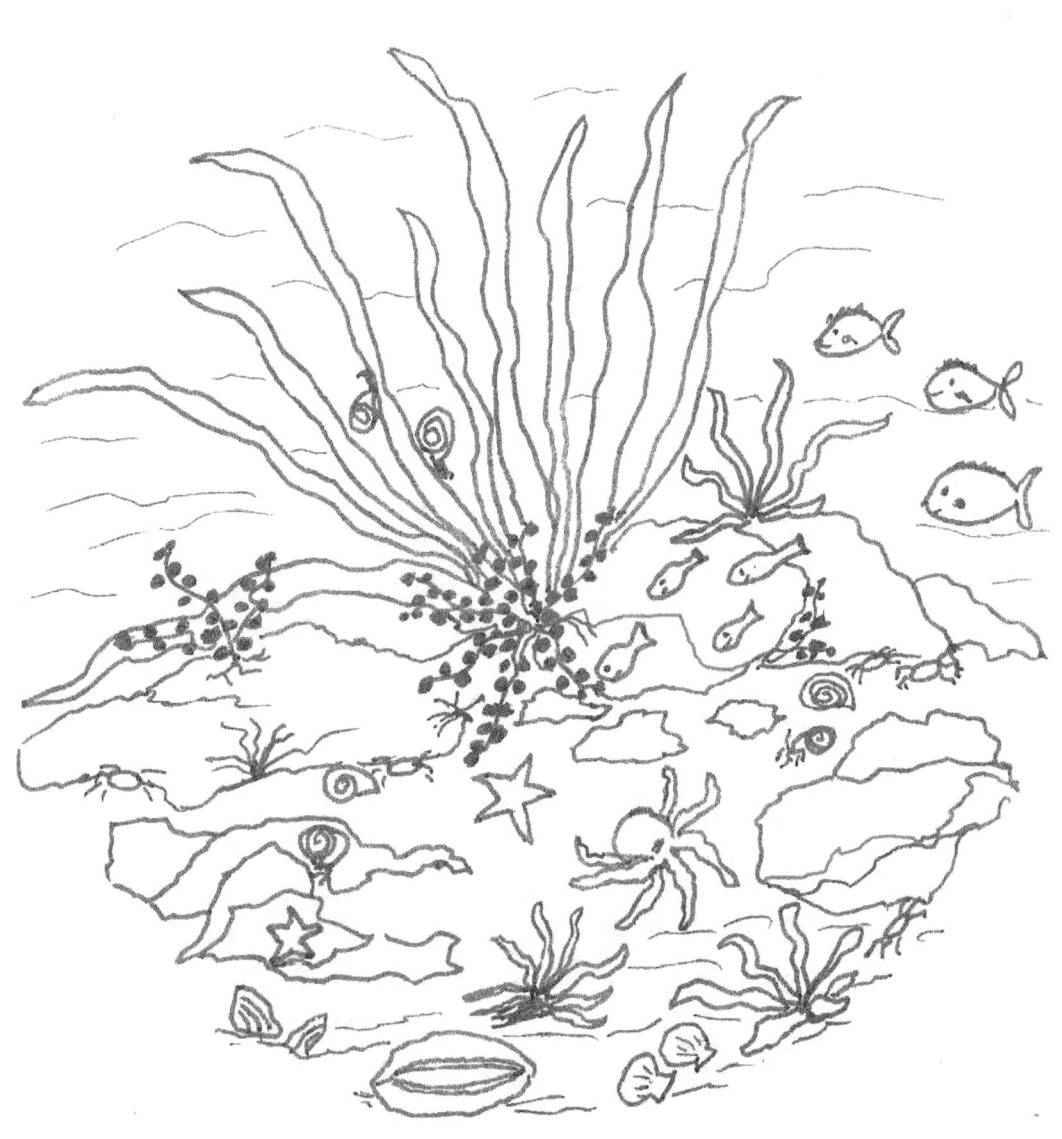

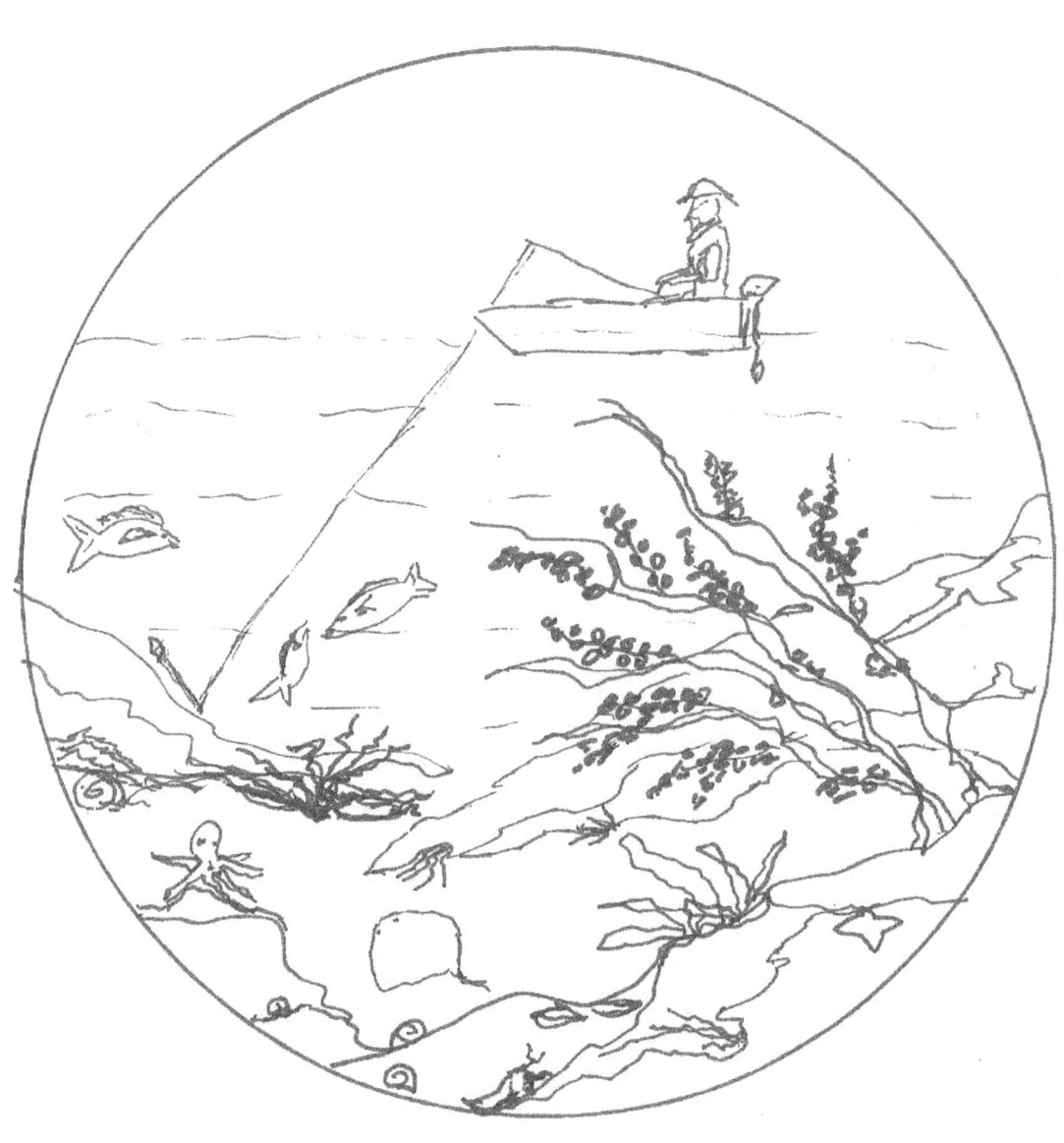

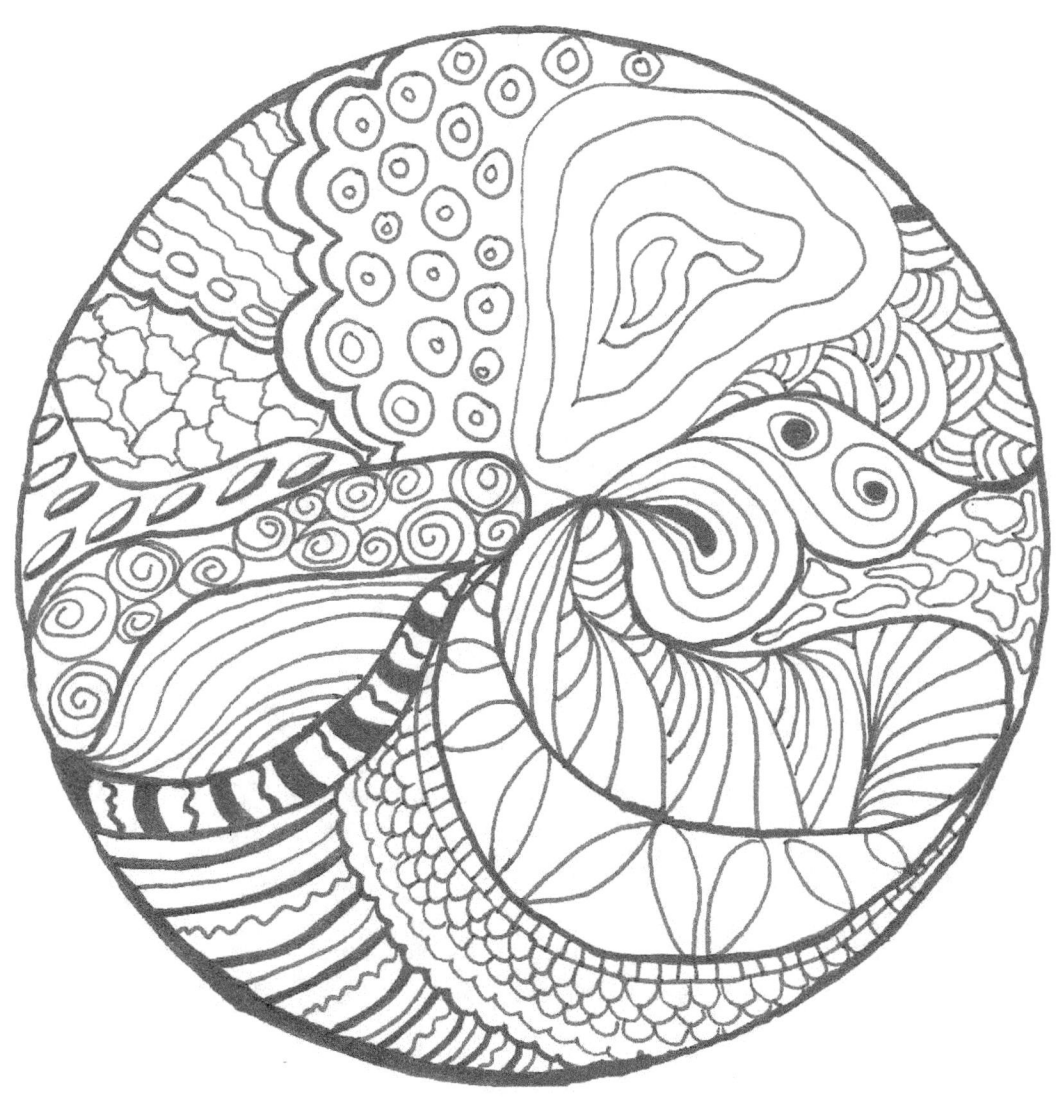

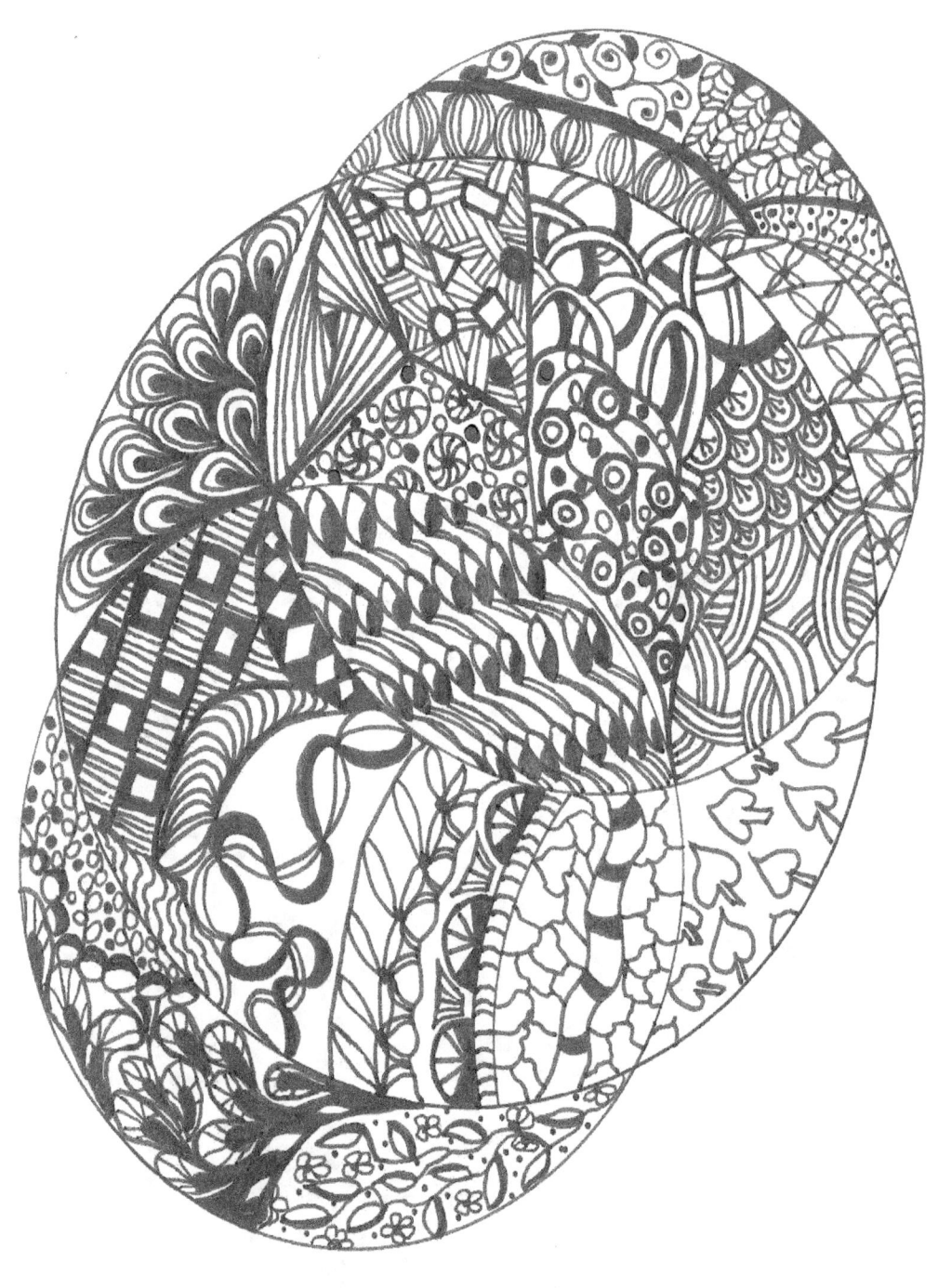

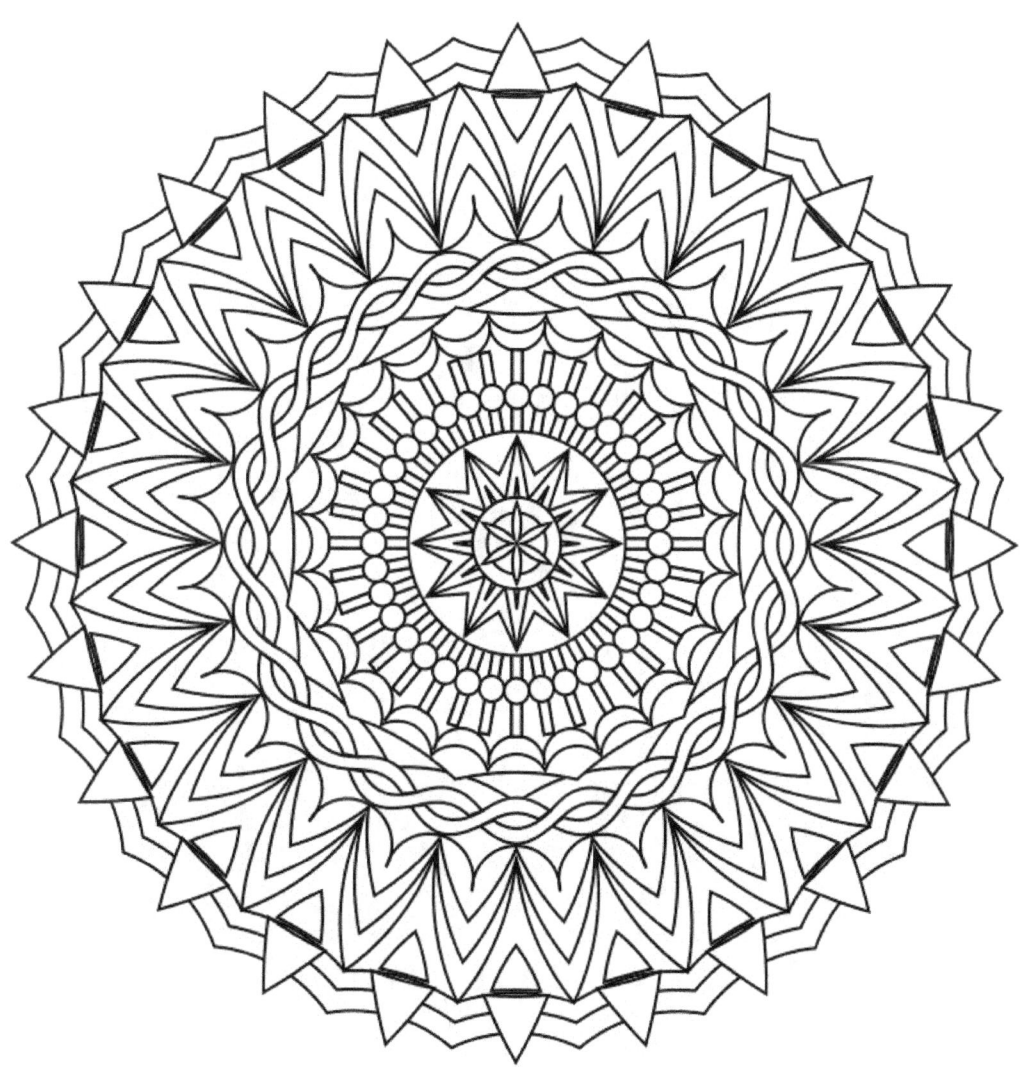

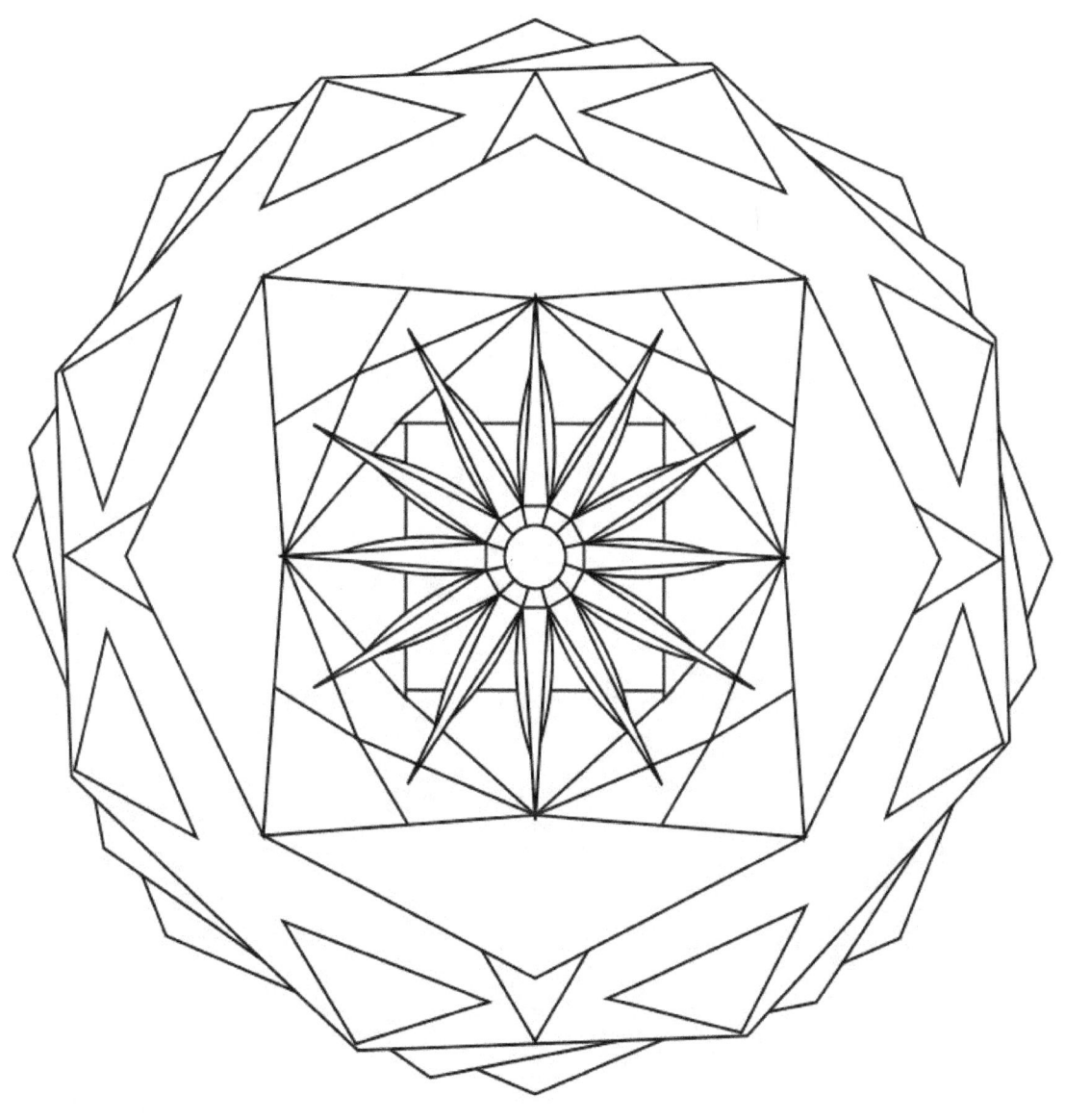

KD COLORING STUDIO

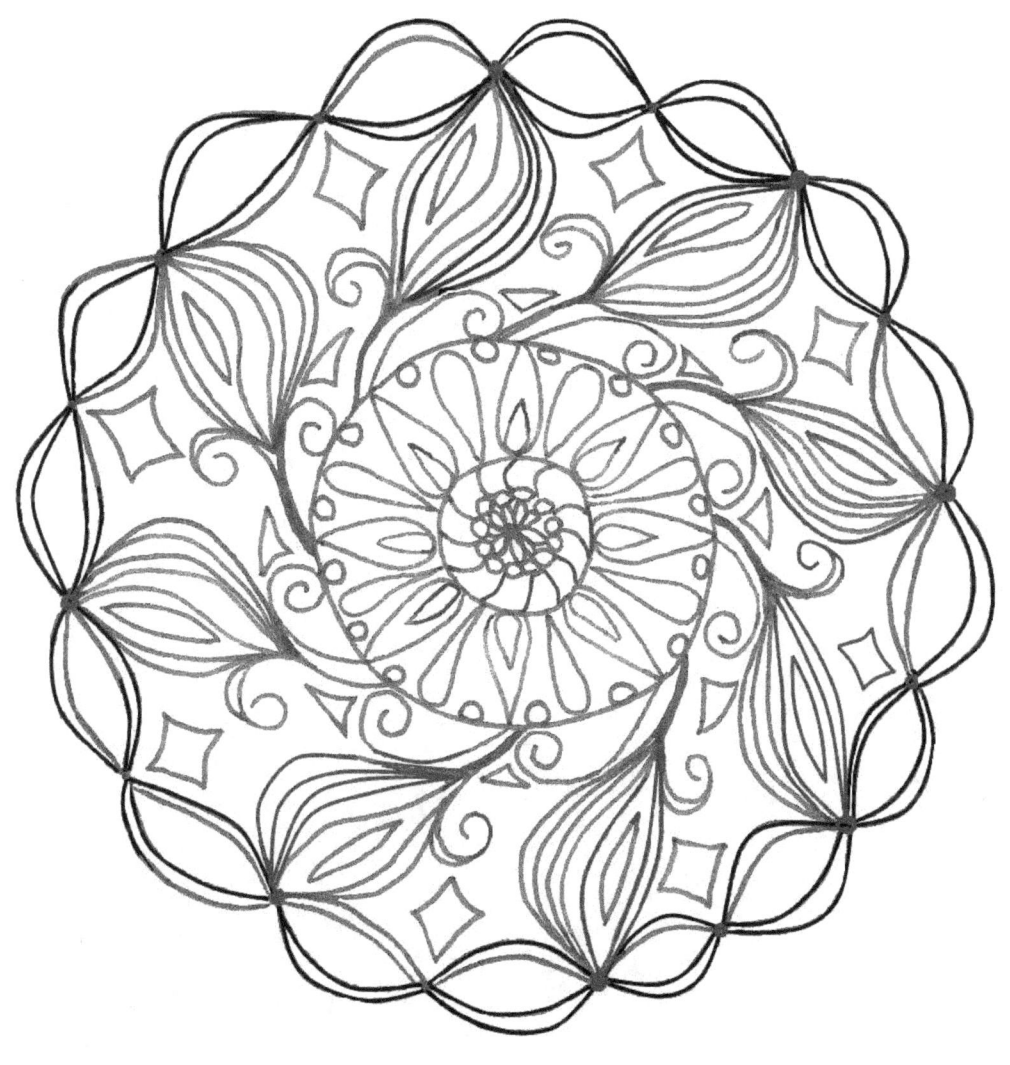

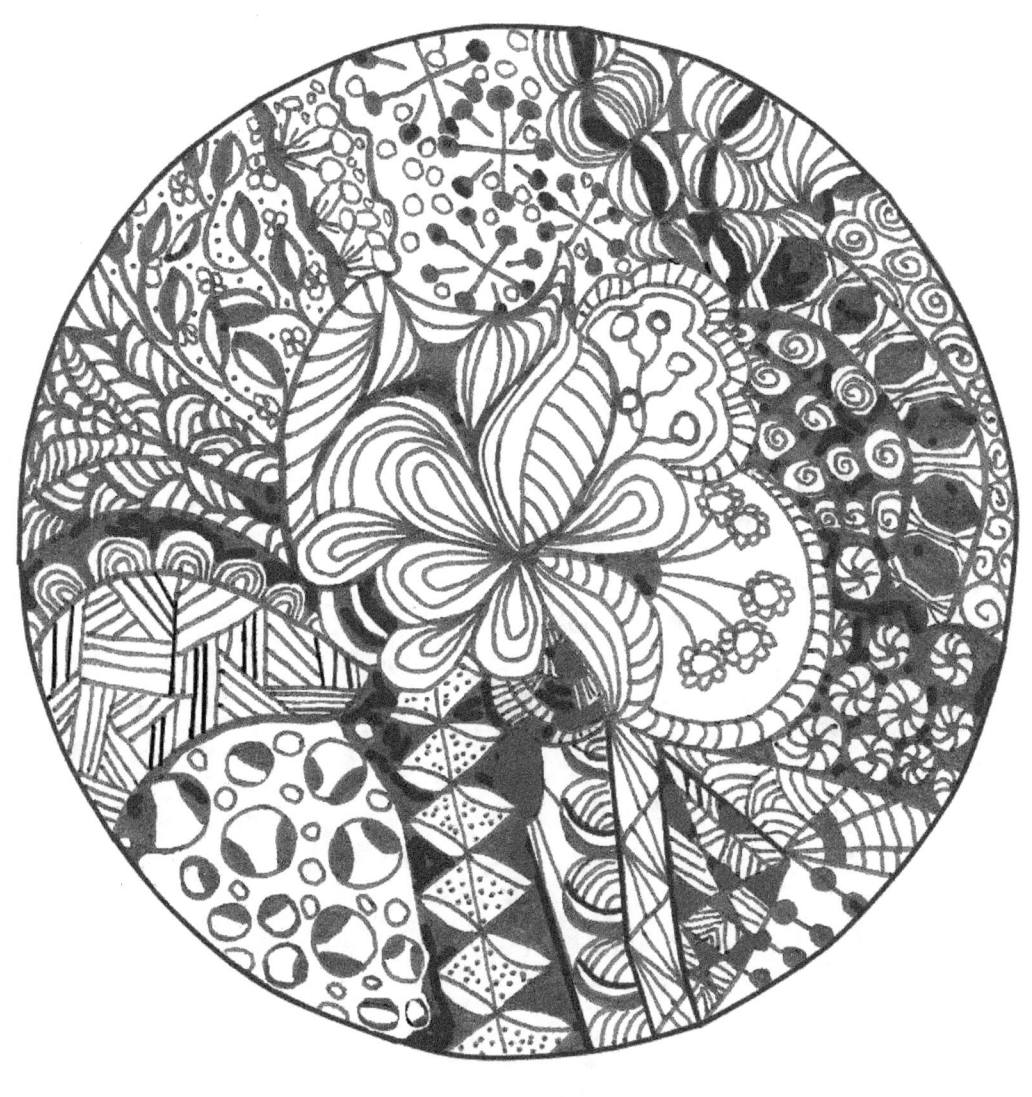

Kaye Dennan

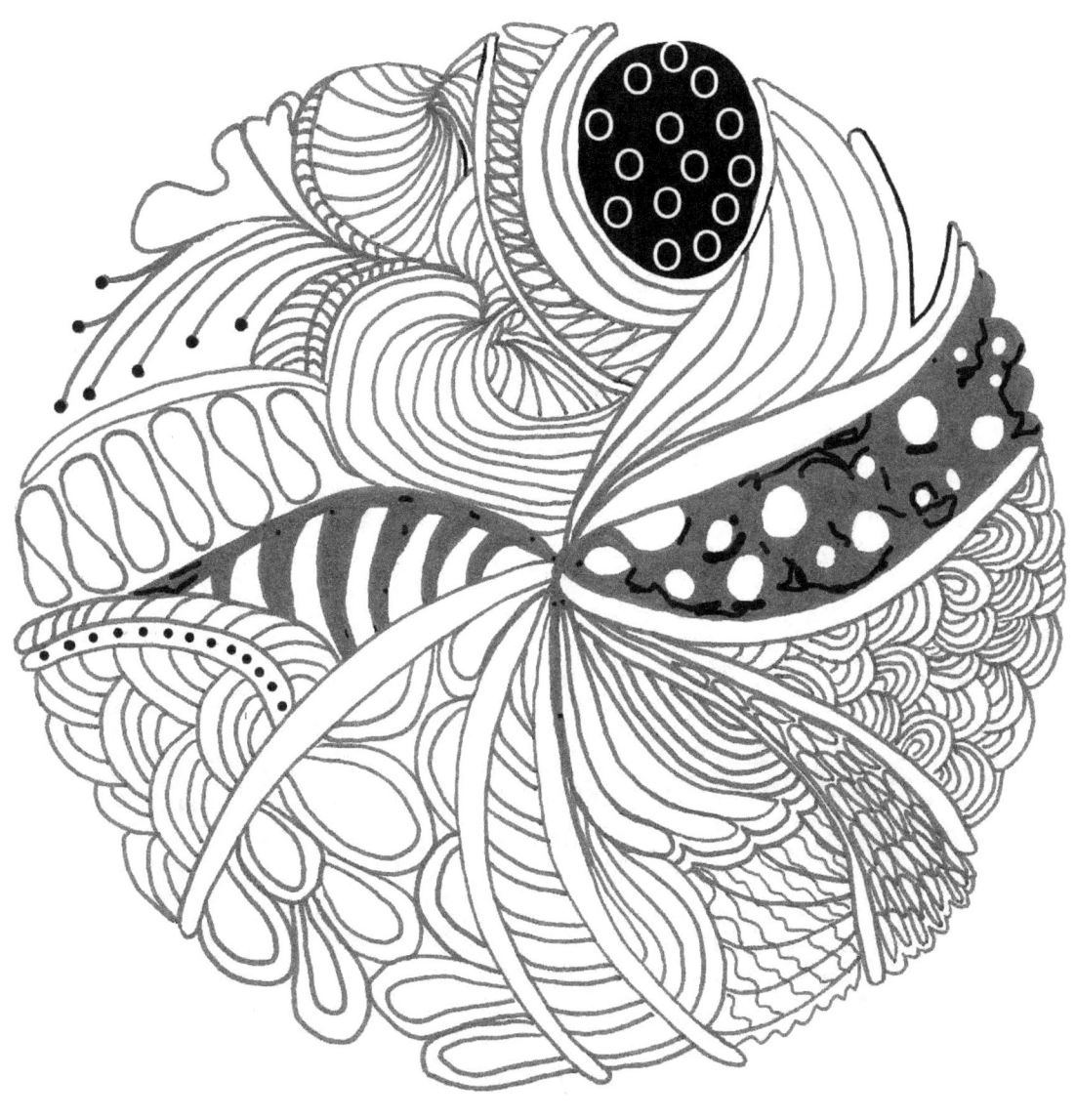

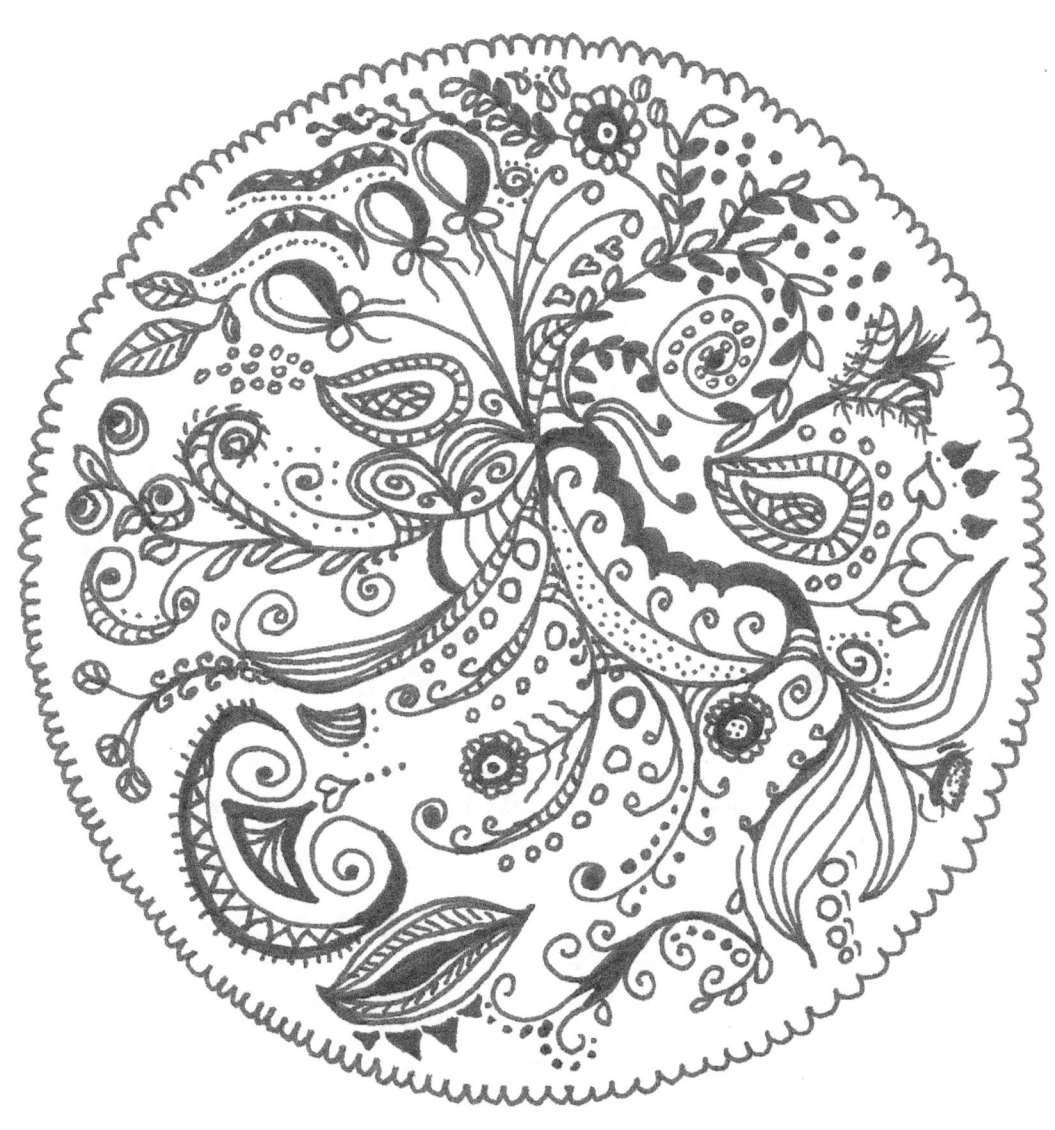

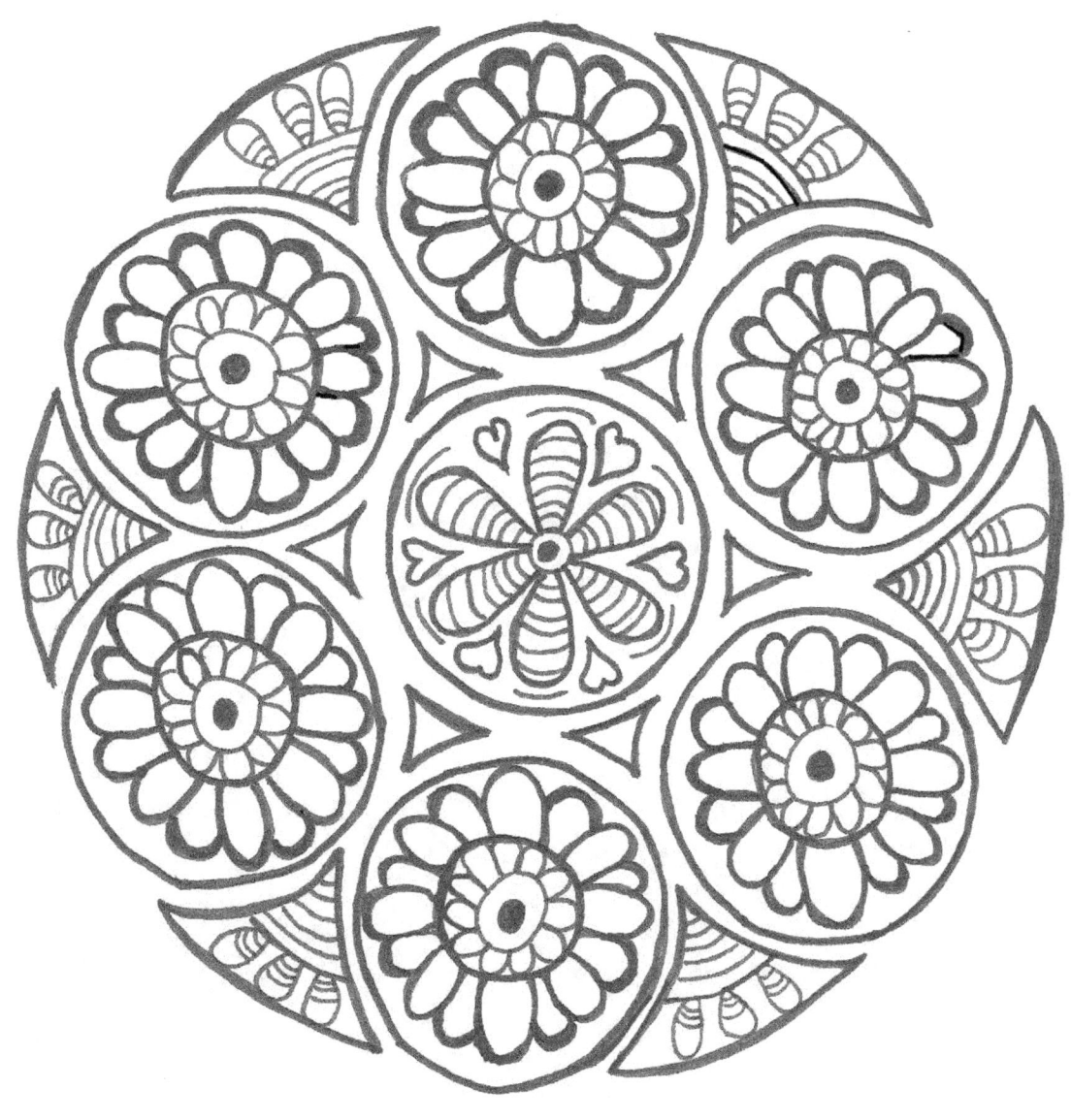

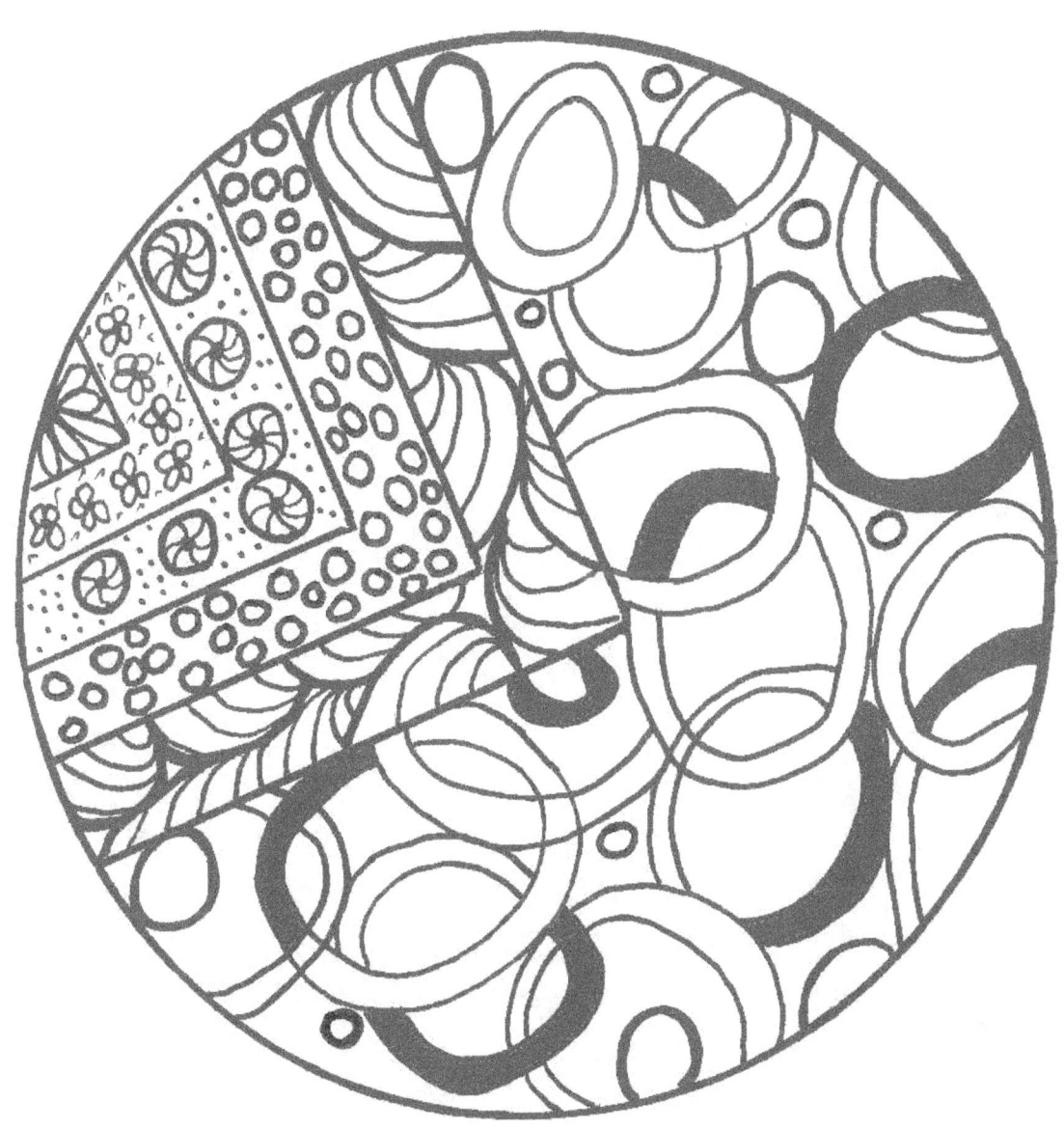

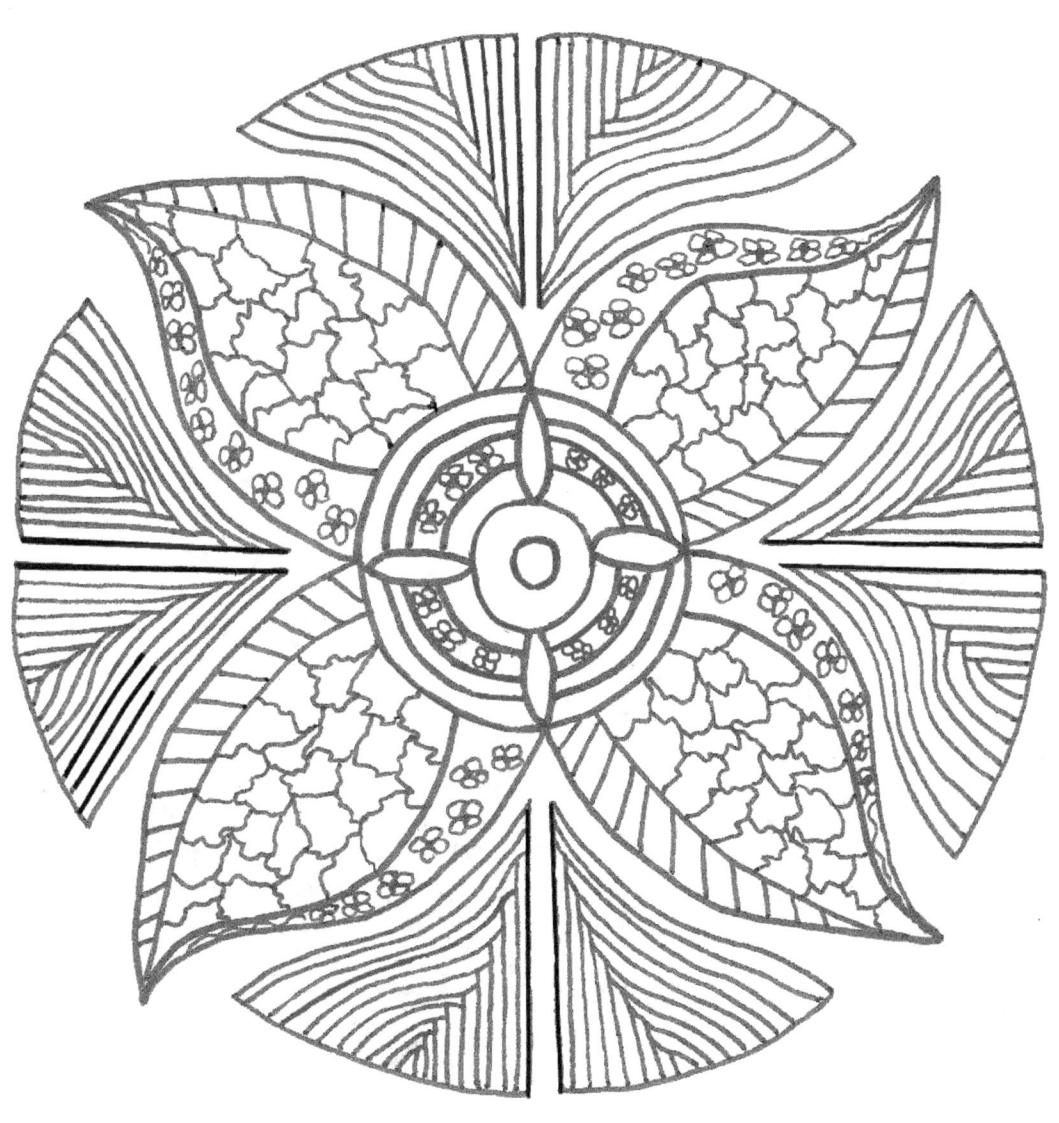

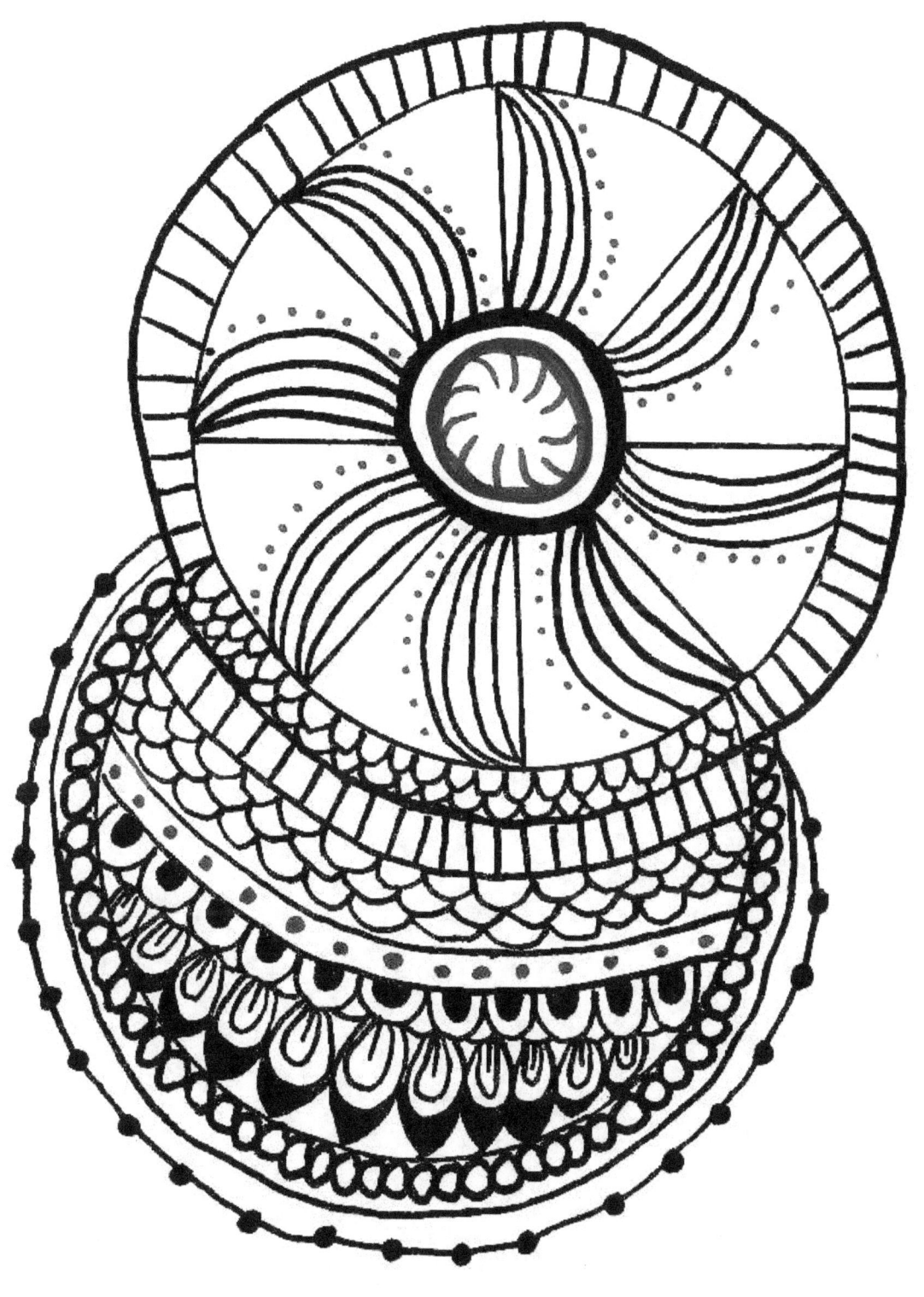

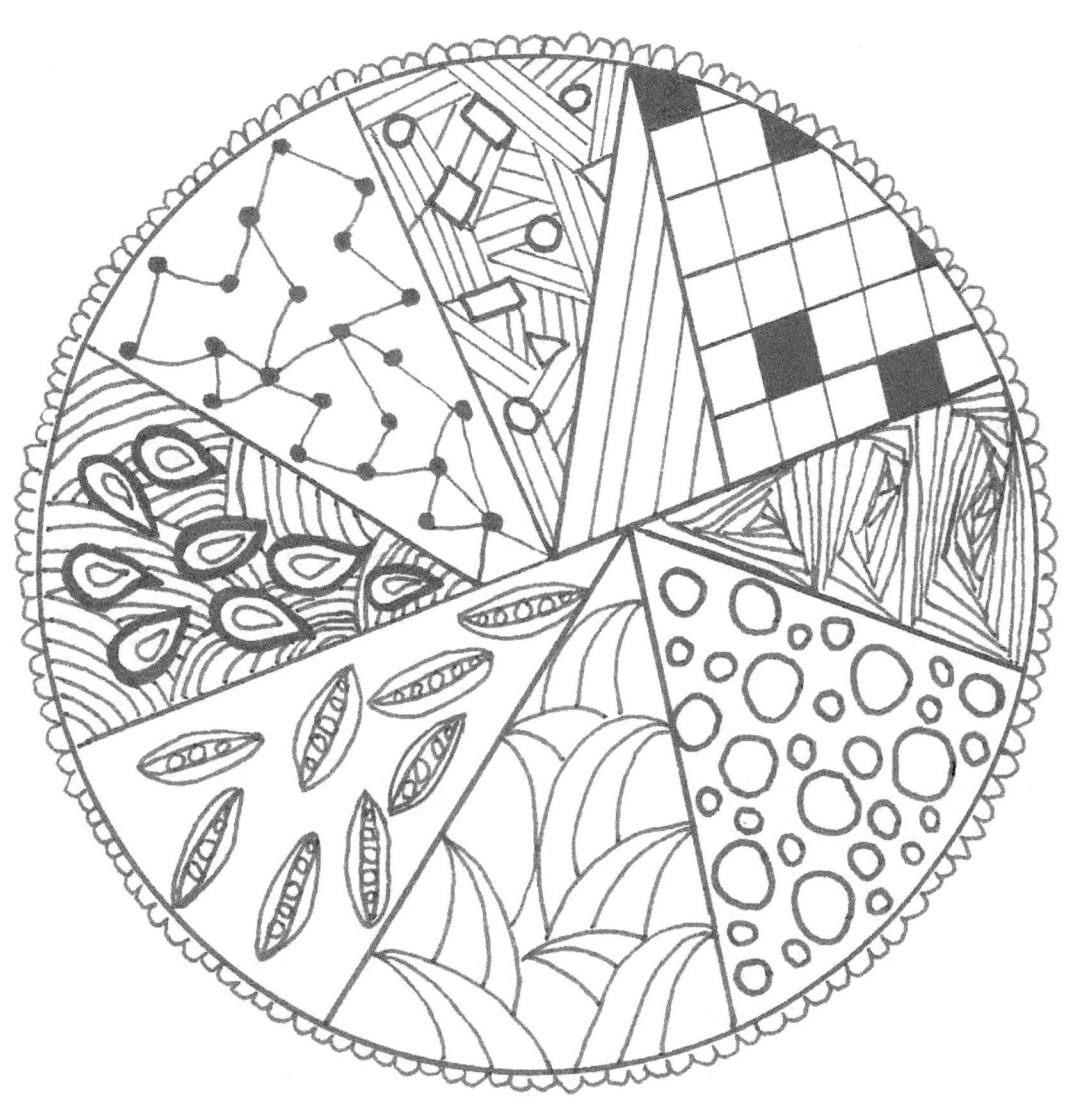

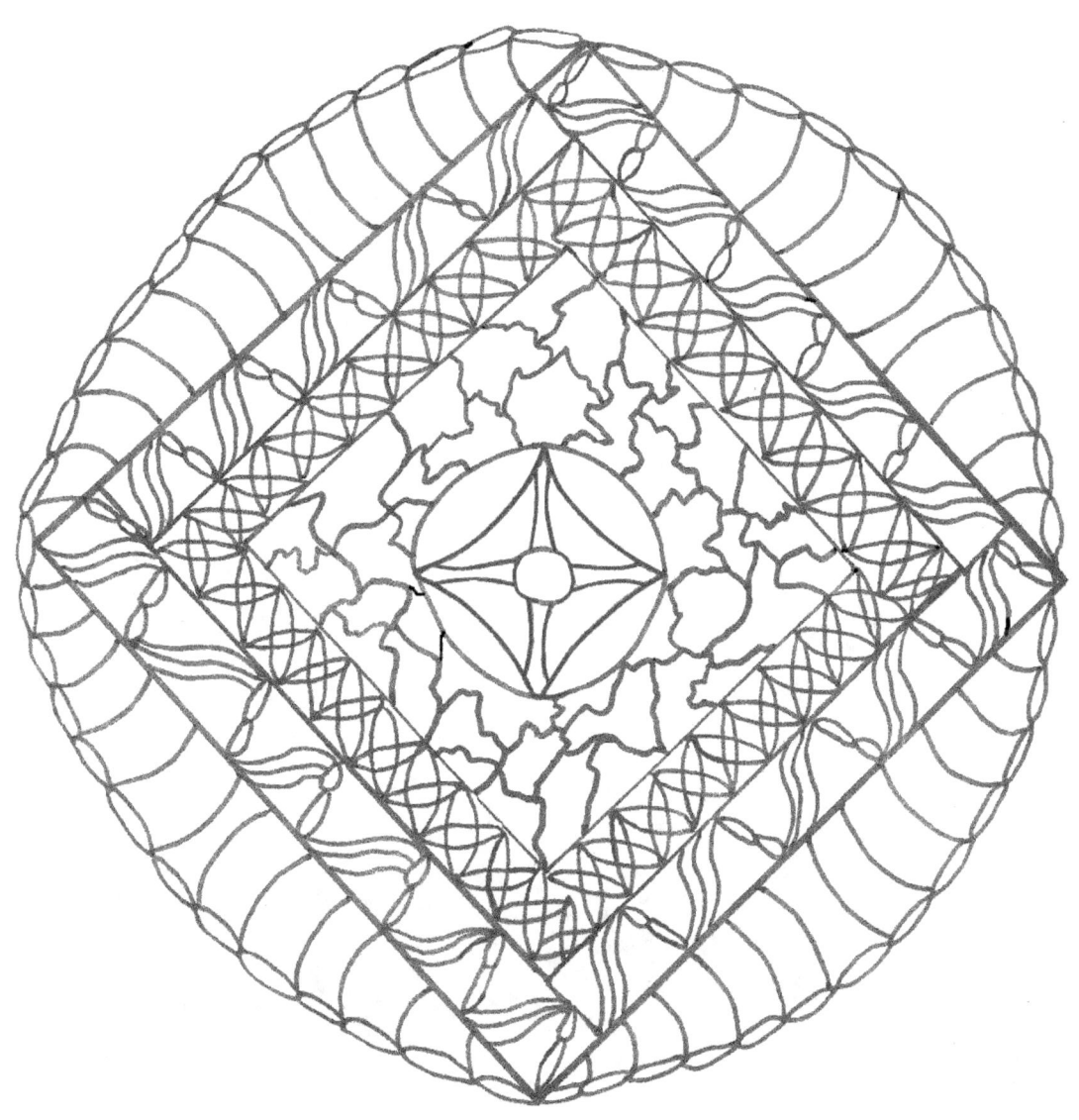

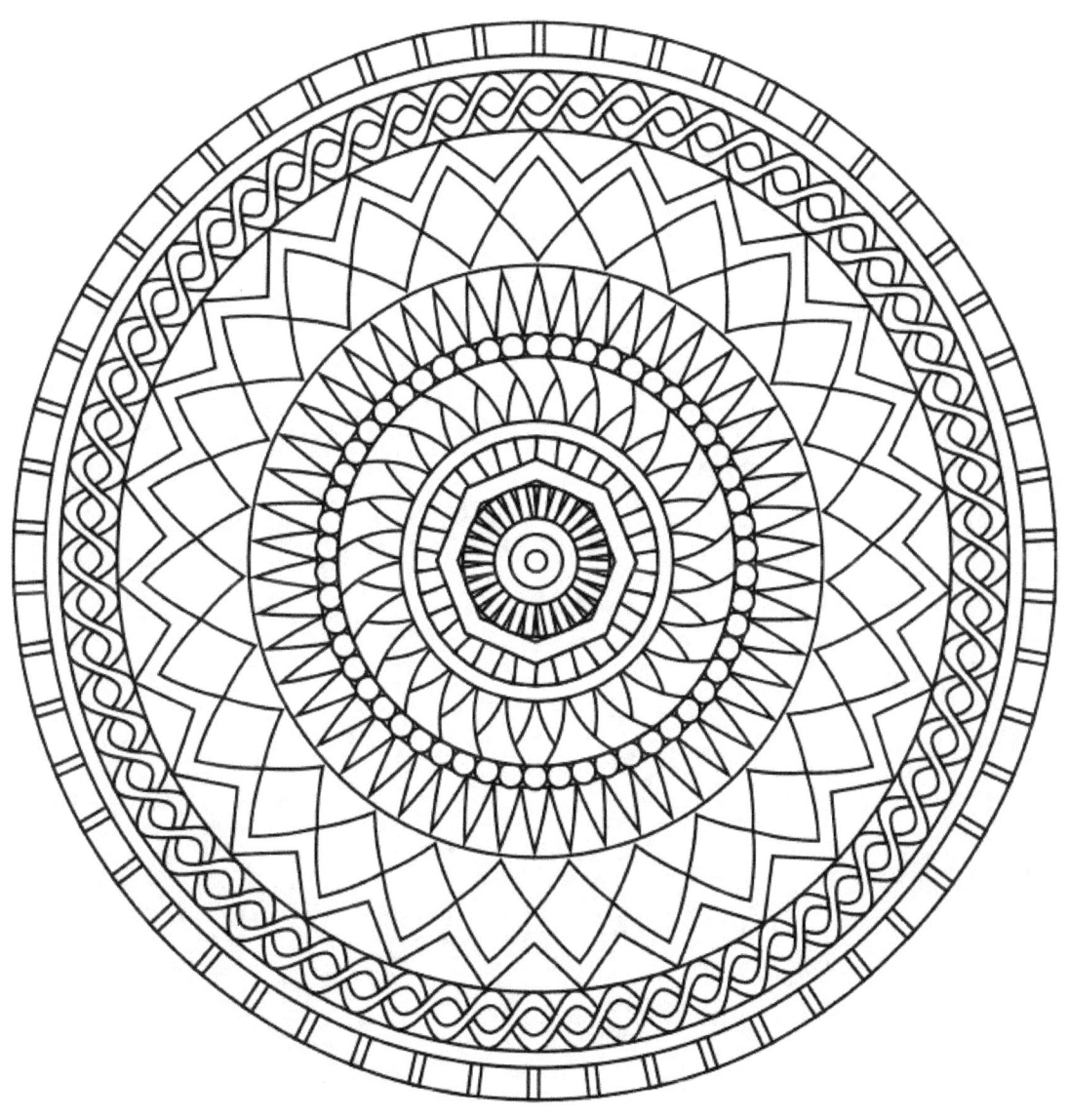

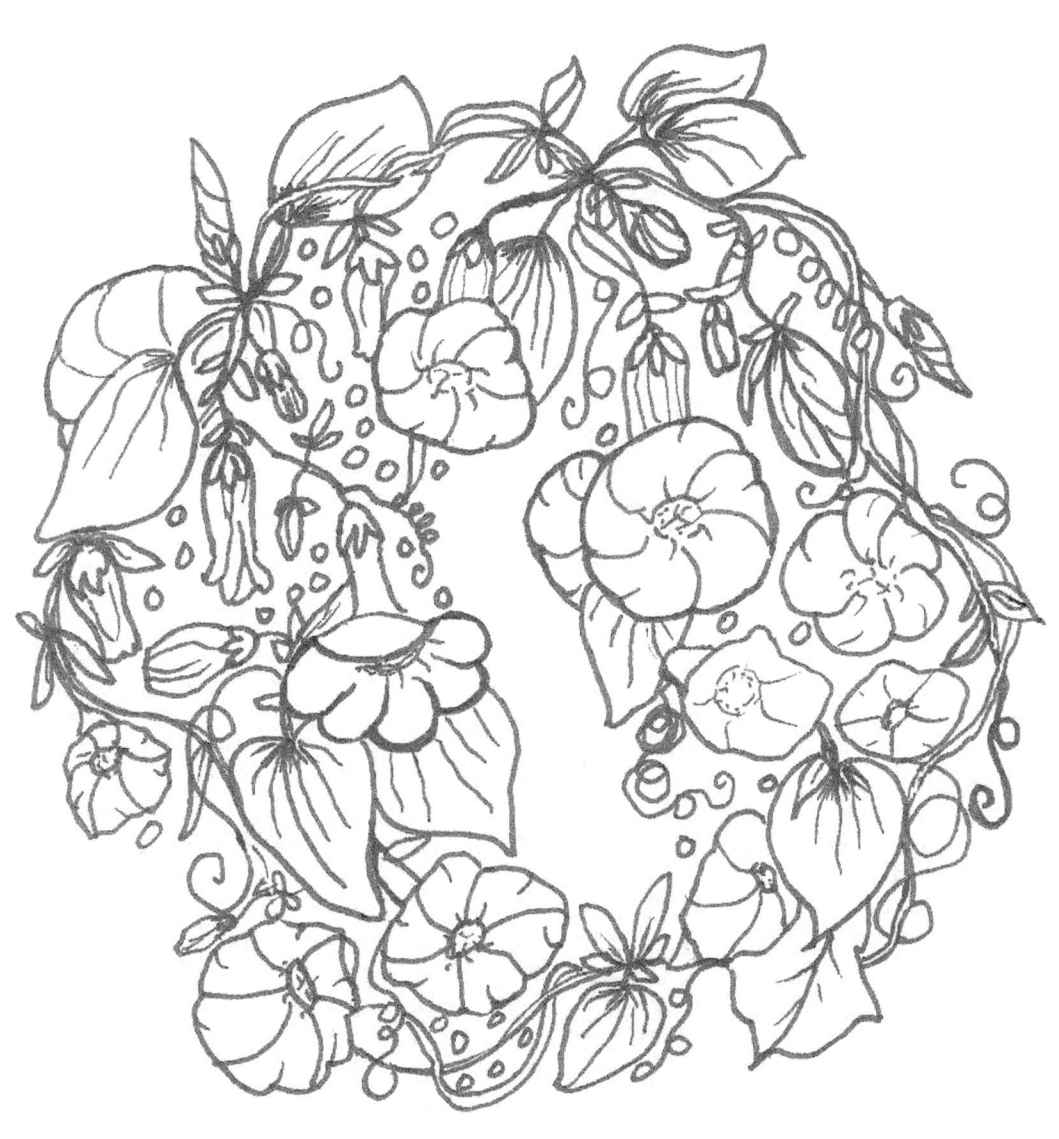

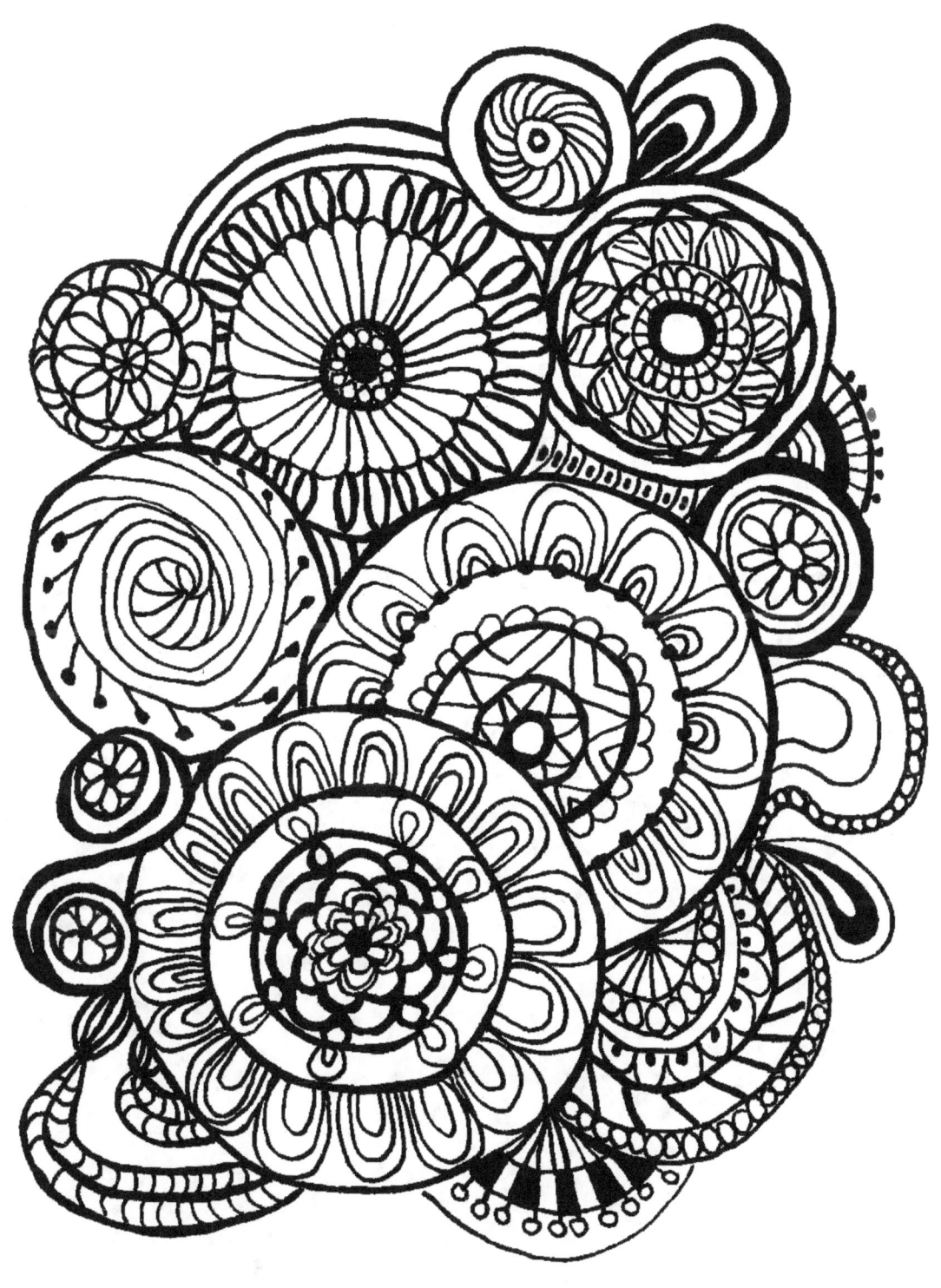

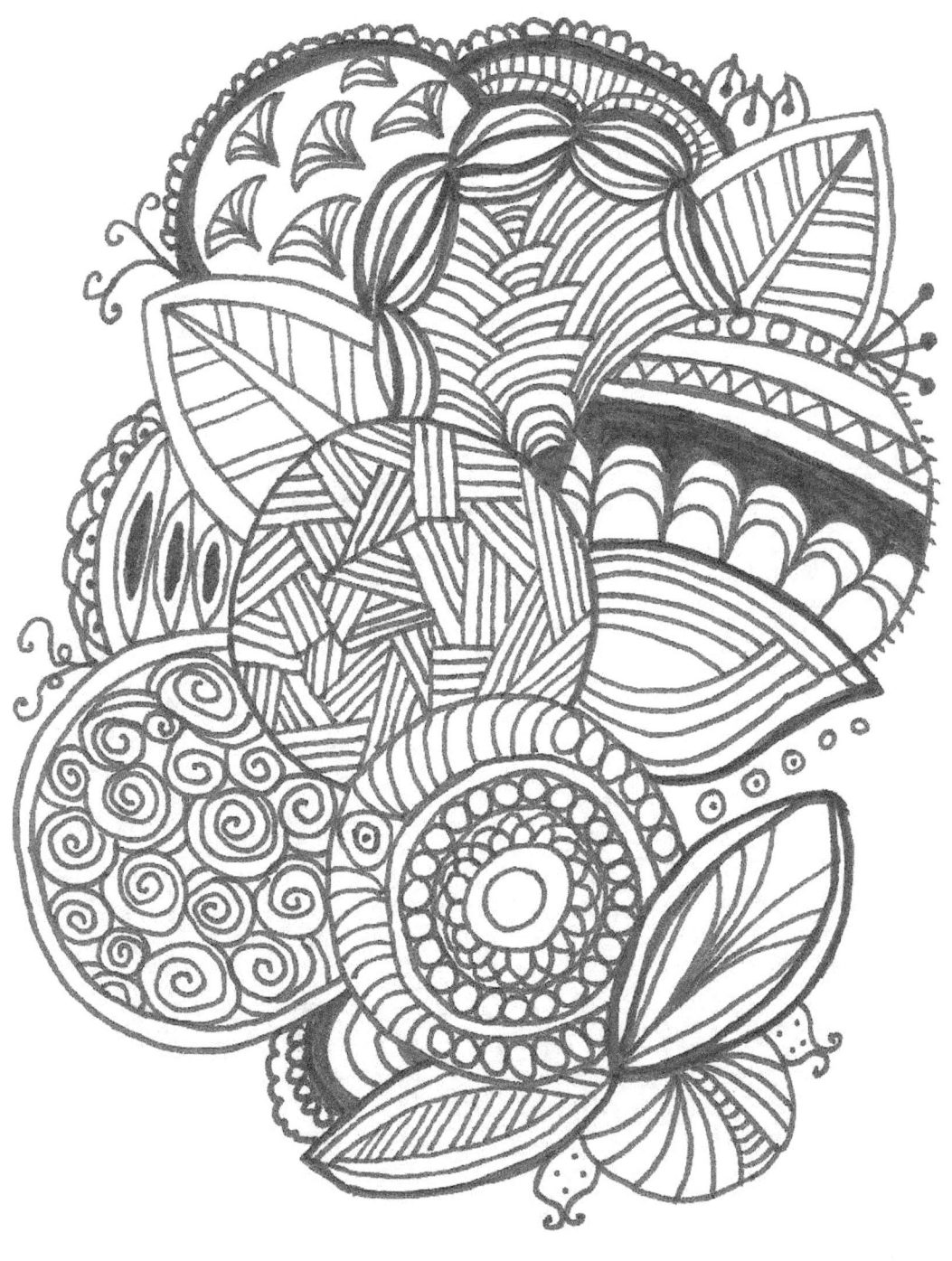

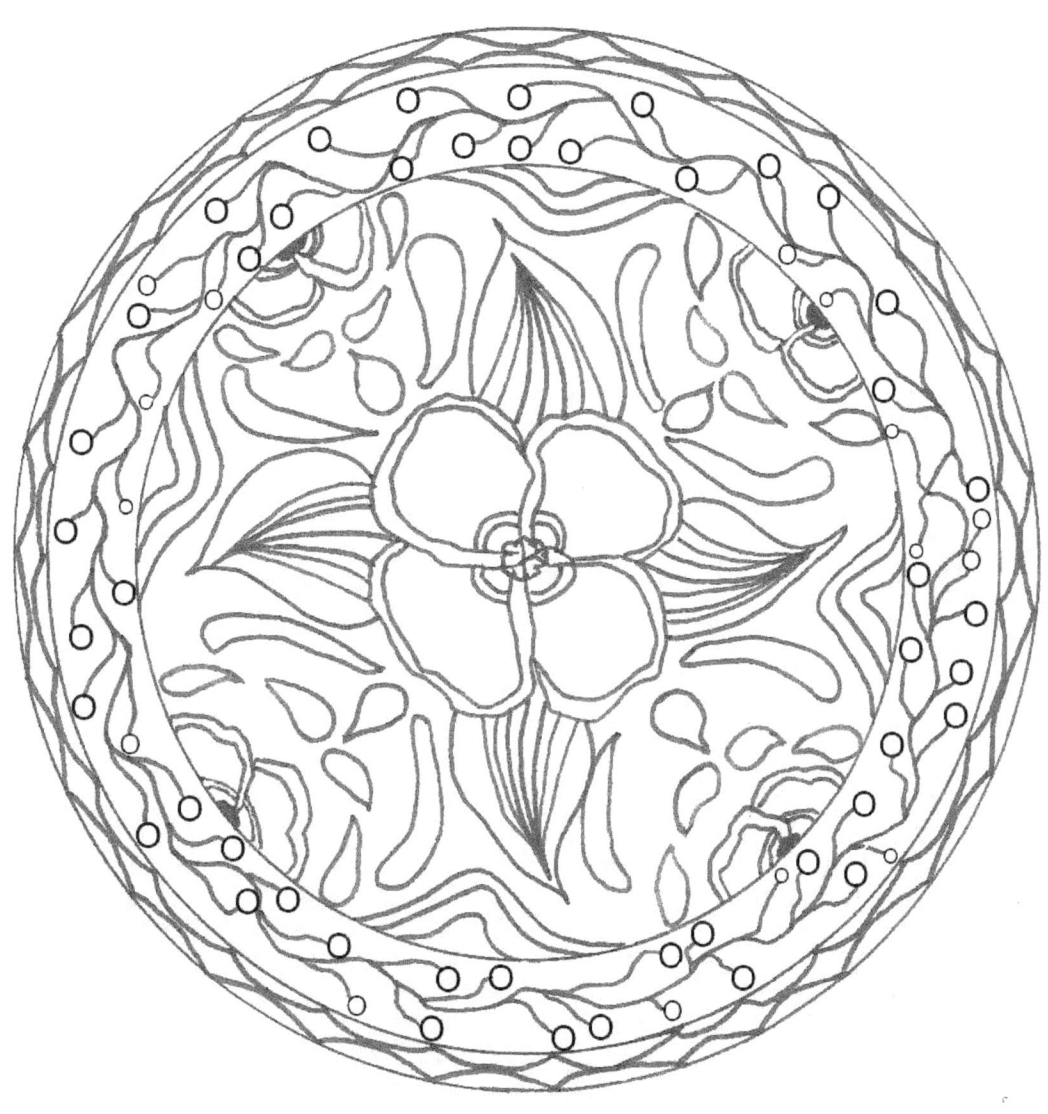

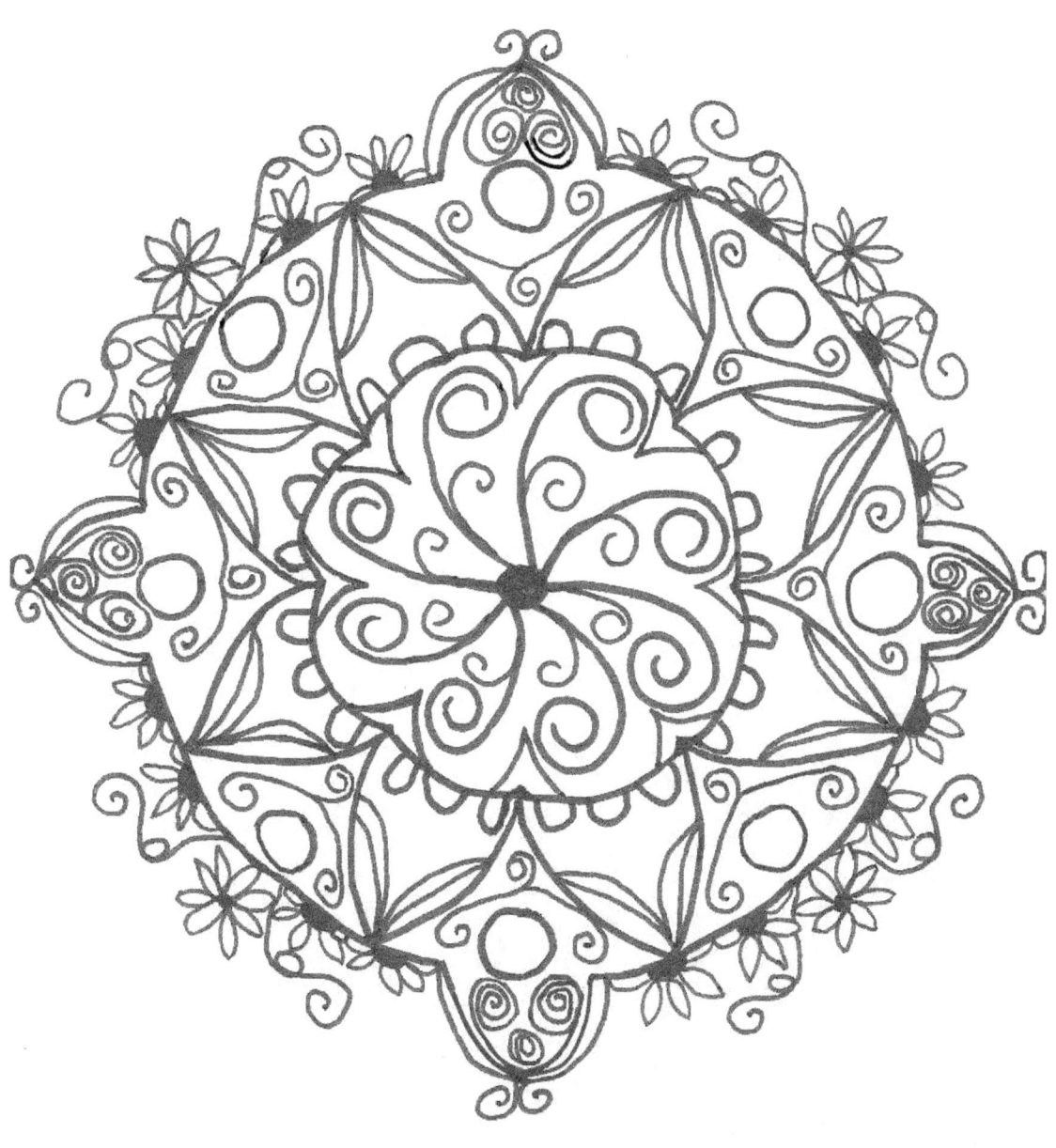

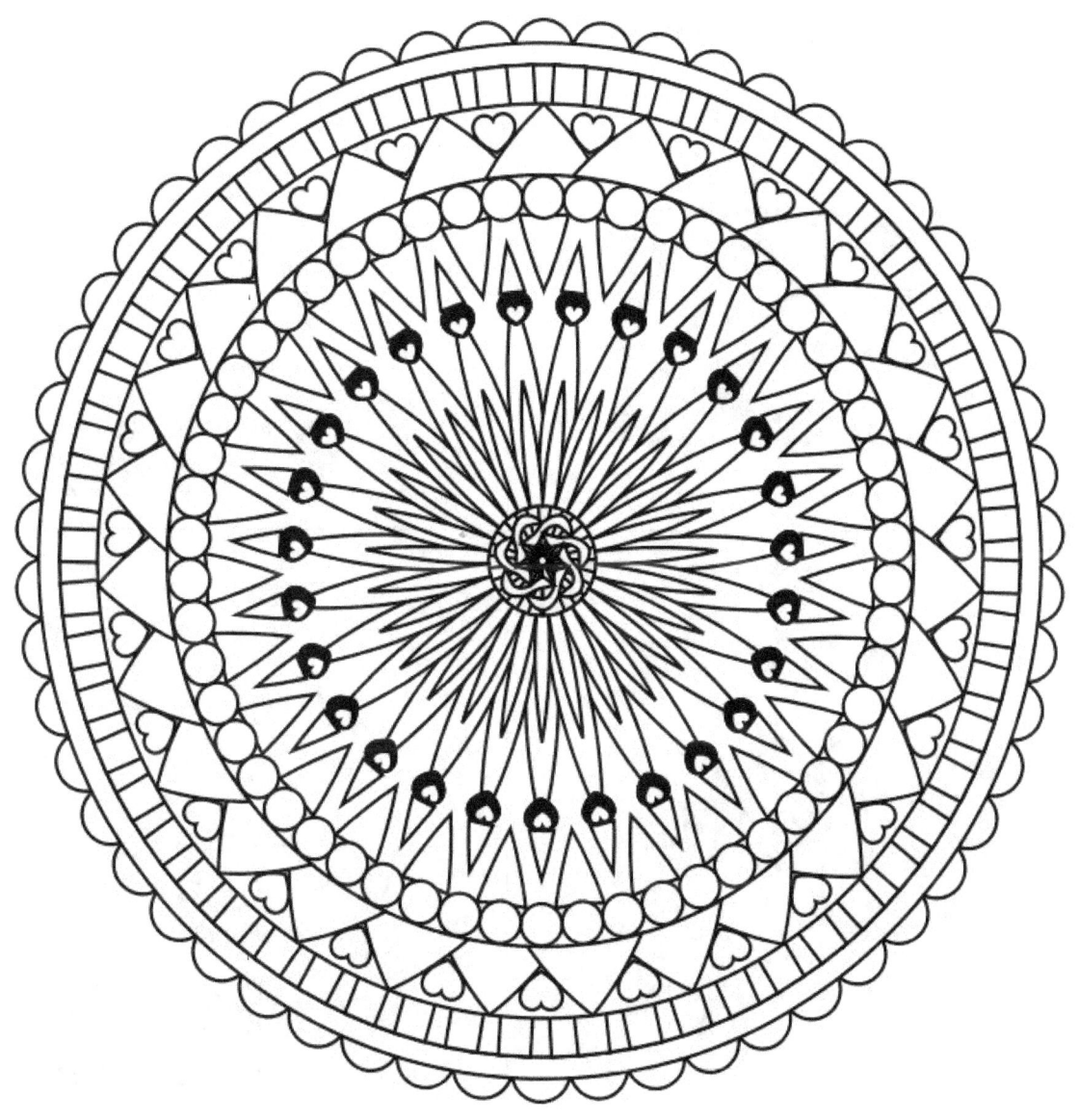

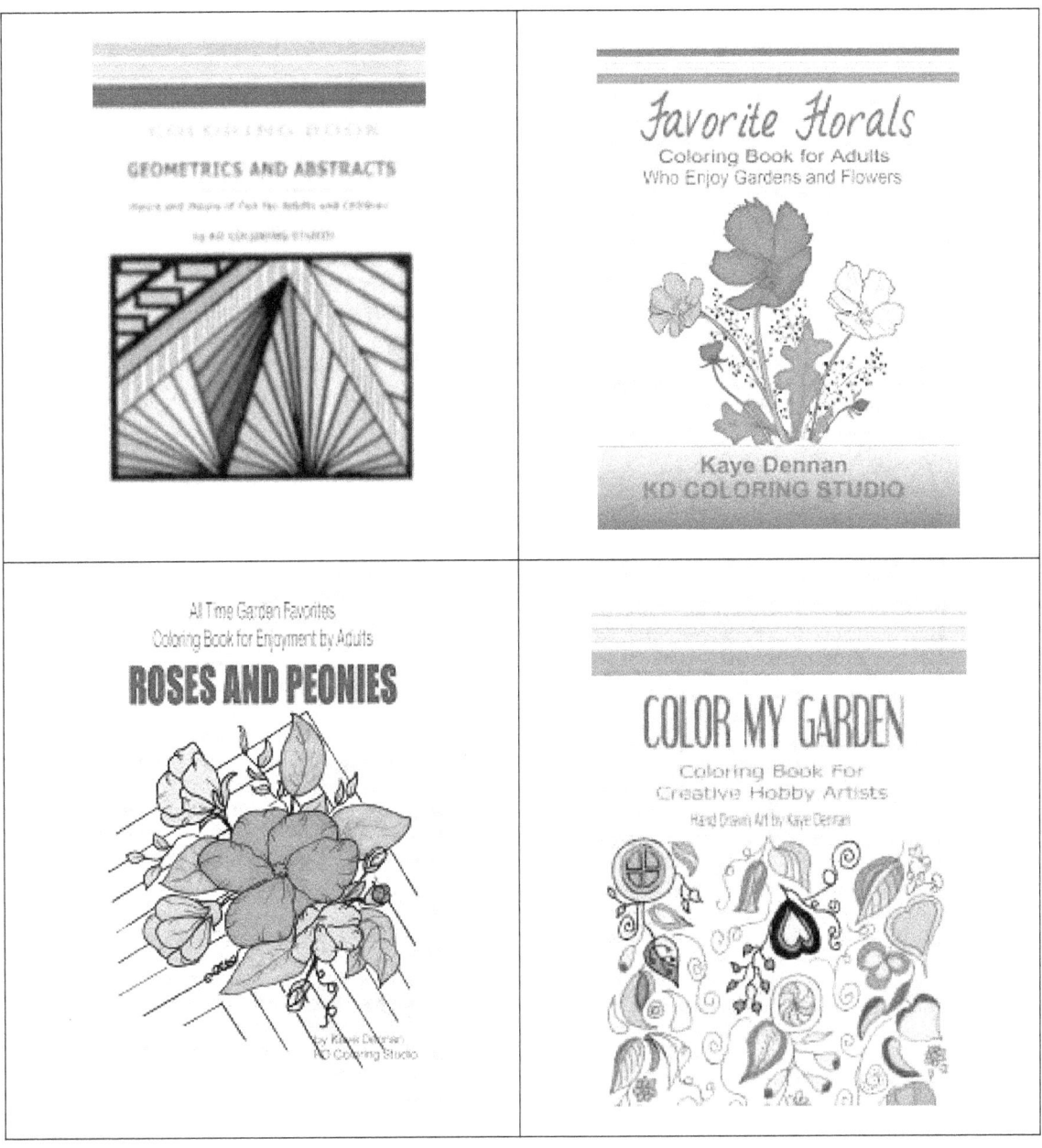

More paperback coloring books can be sourced through

KD COLORING STUDIO AT

http://kdcoloring.com